STRENGTH DRAPED IN A SAREE

10 WOMEN 10 JOURNEYS ONE DREAM

AMBICA MISHRA

Clever Fox® PUBLISHING

Chennai • Bangalore

CLEVER FOX PUBLISHING
Chennai, India

Published by CLEVER FOX PUBLISHING 2025

ISBN: 978-93-7500-428-8

CONTENTS

TESTIMONIALS

In the many lives I've lived in this one life time, Ambica stands out as one of the most impressive minds I have come across during my days as a trainer and a mentor. Sharp, witty, well read, and very aware; Ambica was always as strong in her words as she was in her thoughts.

It's a privilege to see her bring out her debut work, and I wish her the very best going forward, though knowing her, I'm sure she won't need it.

– Bodhayan Roychaudhury, Writer-Director

In a deeply patriarchal world there are women who courageously combat every challenge life tosses at them.

In this collection of profiles, Ambica Mishra ensures their victory will be celebrated by every reader. Their stories will inspire young women who hesitantly stand on the threshold of their dreams and aspirations.

– Payal Mohanka, Journalist

Ambica's book serves as a reminder on several fronts for women. Olympian Paramjeet Choudhary tells us to take out 2 hours daily for your health. Social activist Rekha Sharma's journey shows us that affluent or not, each one of us needs to do something for those in society who don't have a voice. Ecologist

Kaberi Kar Gupta's trajectory reminds us to reconnect with wildlife, instead of spending all our time in this urban jungle.

And for the rest of the reminders, read the book already!

– Kabir Singh Bhandari, Entertainment Editor (Print),

The Free Press Journal

Strength Draped in a Saree is not just a book, it's a mirror held up to the strength of every woman today. It beautifully shows how a woman can remain rooted in tradition while soaring in ambition. These stories remind us that there is truly nothing a woman cannot achieve once she sets her mind to it and often, the depth of her strength surprises even her. This book speaks to the countless women who quietly juggle dreams, careers, families, and identities every single day. I truly believe this should be read by every young girl as well, as an early reminder that her possibilities are limitless.

– Sanjana Bhajanka,

India's First Certified Baby Planner,

Author, Entrepreneur

A LETTER TO THE READERS

When I first heard about "Strength Draped in a Saree", I was deeply moved by the essence of the book. It is a heartfelt collection that celebrates real women who turn their struggles into strength and their pain into purpose.

Each story is a tribute to the everyday resilience in the lives of women - resilience that defines feminine energy in its truest form.

Ambica Mishra has beautifully captured what it means to be a woman in today's world: balancing roles, breaking barriers, and still holding on to compassion and grace.

Through her words, we meet women who remind us that empowerment is not about being loud, but about being authentic - finding greatness in the everyday.

As an artist, I've always believed that stories have the power to heal, to connect, and to inspire. "Strength Draped in a Saree" does all of that and more. It speaks to the heart and makes you pause, reflect, and admire the quiet power of women who very nonchalantly carry great responsibilities on their shoulders.

This book is a celebration of womanhood - women who are draped not just in fabric, but in dignity, courage, and love. I congratulate Ambica for creating something so meaningful and timeless.

Raashii Khanna, Actress
Mumbai
November 2025

FOREWORD TO THE BOOK

When I joined IIM Ahmedabad, I was expected to bring with me two sarees, to be worn at formal occasions. The list of such occasions included the annual corporate dinner, placement interviews and even, the convocation.

Three decades later, at the Institute's annual convocation, not a single girl can be spotted in a saree. Each one is wearing a standard business suit, and thinks of it as 'power dressing'. And I feel sad, because that is so shallow an idea.

Strength lies not in one's attire but in one's attitude, and actions.

It lies in the calloused hands of the lady in a nylon sari, tucked at the waist, running a Chinese street food stall to support her family.

Strength lies within the Koli fisherwoman who travels up and down Mumbai locals, balancing a basket on her head in a navvari (nine-yard saree).

The young mother whose education was cut short due to Covid but, nevertheless, posts reels on Instagram filled with positivity.

Most of these women wear saree not out of choice but societal expectations, which is why those who have a choice rebel against it and wear anything but. And herein lies the eternal dilemma:

"Staying true to your roots and yet embracing modernity."

This book features the stories of women who have made these choices, and found that balance. They fought for their dreams, without being strident and created a path to personal progress, carrying their families along with them.

Indeed, these stories will appeal to women, young and old, for so many of us have faced this struggle. As well as any man who wants to understand the women in their lives. Trust me; it will open your eyes.

I wish Ambica Mishra the very best for her debut as an author. May this book find a wide and varied audience. So that the next time you see a woman in a saree, you look beyond the obvious, and see her inner strength.

Rashmi Bansal
Mumbai
November 2025

Dedicated to the three of Women who mean pride, endeavor and compassion to me:

My Grandmother Late Smt Sumitra Prashar, My Mother Mrs Renu Prashar

& My Mother in Law Mrs Anita Sampat Mishra

ABOUT THE AUTHOR

Ambica Mishra is a proud alumna of La Martiniere for Girls, Kolkata, the school that shaped not just her education but her character. At La Martiniere, courage was not taught it was lived. Confidence was not inherited-it was earned. The school encouraged young girls to speak their minds, stand their ground and dream beyond boundaries.

Ambica grew up in a close-knit and hardworking family, with a younger sister Radhika, and no brothers. It was a house where values were grounded in honesty and resilience. Her parents were first generation entrepreneurs in Kolkata. They built Mazel Boutique, a designer house, through sheer determination. They made countless sacrifices so their children would never feel the weight of limitation. They did not teach Ambica or Radhika to chase success-they taught them to deserve it.

From them, she learned resilience, gratitude and the strength to rise every time life demanded it. From her father, who was a philanthropist at heart, she learned that the art of giving wasn't limited to someone's pockets, but to the heart. From her mother she picked up logic, practicality and a great zeal for life even at the toughest of times.

Among the people who greatly influenced her formative years were Mrs. Sarkar, then the Vice Principal and now the Principal of La Martiniere for Girls. She wasn't just an educator, she was a presence. Elegant in thought and firm in discipline, she brought grace to authority and dignity to leadership. Apart from being an eloquent and well versed teacher, Ma'am Sarkar went beyond books to impart life lessons to students, which Ambica still remembers. She showed Ambica that a woman could be strong without being loud, and powerful without being intimidating.

She graduated from J.D. Birla Institute, where she had the honour of being mentored by Dr. Suman Kumar Mukerjee, renowned economist, scholar and extraordinary educator. He was more than a professor, he was an institution in himself. He often reminded his students, "There are no free lunches in this world, " a truth Ambica carries even today. He taught her discipline of thought, clarity of purpose, and the dignity of hard work. Though he is no longer with us, his voice still echoes in her mind, and his teachings shape her decisions even today. That is the mark of a great teacher-they do not live in classrooms; they live in their students forever. She carries his guidance like a compass-silently, firmly, always pointing her towards purpose.

Ambica went on to pursue her MBA at Calcutta Business School, where she met a mentor who profoundly shaped her individuality, then Professor and now writer-director Mr. Bodhayan Roychaudhury (Bodhy Sir). He often called her a misfit, and what once puzzled her eventually empowered her. Being a misfit meant she didn't just follow a path, she carved one. He gave her the courage to ask questions that others avoided and to embrace a voice that was fearlessly her own.

She graduated with four gold medals, and in the same year, she married Mr. Ankit Mishra. Her convocation day remains etched in her heart as a moment of pride-her parents and in-laws stood by her, celebrating not just her success, but her journey.

Ankit has been her greatest mirror, reflecting truth, not comfort. As an industrialist he has always guided her with his strong intuition and forward thinking attitude. Where she was emotional and idealistic, he brought clarity and logic, where society showed her a convenient illusion; he showed her the reality behind it. Their worlds are different, yet beautifully aligned. She often says, "We carve our own paths in life, but whenever those paths cross, the world will witness magic-where the lamb walks beside the lion, and love leads them both."

Marriage did not limit her, it expanded her horizons. It gave her depth, emotional intelligence and the strength to evolve without losing herself. She comes from a lineage of strong women-her mother, grandmother and mother-in-law-women are women with great compassion and diligence. Ambica believes that her daughter will inherit the same strength and willpower that she did. She will not inherit sacrifice; she will inherit choice. She will not inherit fear; she will inherit freedom.

As a writer, Ambica believes words are not ink-they are energy. She writes for every woman who has ever been told she is too much or not enough. She writes so that forgotten dreams find courage again. She writes so that every woman who reads her work remembers: she is extraordinary. Ambica believes every woman carries both Durga and Shiva within-creation and destruction, intuition and power, stillness and storm.

With over 15 years of experience as a Soft Skills Educator, Corporate Trainer and Certified NLP Coach, Ambica has trained students, professionals, entrepreneurs and leaders across industries. She doesn't believe in motivational speaking-she believes in transformation through truth. Her work focuses on helping people find their voice, build inner courage and lead with purpose.

Her mission is to awaken the power within every woman-to help her rise, rebuild, and reclaim her story with dignity, courage and unshakable belief.

PROLOGUE

Once in our lives, there comes a moment of realization that makes us ponder what we have given back to society. For me, it came as the question -What is the legacy I want to leave behind in this world?

Would it be a company, a piece of jewellery, or a few words of advice? What do I truly hold within me that I can pass on - to my children, to the women of generations to come, and to those around me who know me? A book.

My father always told me, "People can take away your wealth, your home, your property - you can lose all of these with your own hands. But nobody can ever take away your knowledge. Nobody can snatch away your education."

Those words stayed with me. I wanted to use this asset - years of learning, living, and observing - to write.

Each day as the morning sun filters softly through the curtains. In that golden light, a woman stands before her mirror, carefully adjusting the pleats of her saree. The world outside is just beginning to stir - the faint whistle of a pressure cooker, the sound of a broom brushing against the floor, a child calling out for breakfast, a husband calling out for tea. For some, answerscripts are stacked on a table, for others some medical reports, for some there are the case files, and for others a stack of laundry waiting to be ironed.

She adjusts her pallu once more, takes a deep breath, and looks at herself. In the reflection, she doesn't see a housewife, a teacher, or a manager. She sees a woman who will carry the weight of the day, quietly, competently, and beautifully. She carries this weight with great pride though. She likes being called a super woman.

That's how most Indian mornings begin - not with declarations of ambition, but with the silent courage of women who rise before the world does, to cook, to clean, to work.

Each one of them ties her hair, tucks her saree, and steps into a thousand roles - mother, daughter, wife, leader, teacher, healer, entrepreneur -each role stitched invisibly to the other. And yet, somehow, she manages to be all of them without losing herself completely. She may not think of herself as extraordinary, but she is.

There's a teacher somewhere, sipping her tea before school begins, ironing her cotton saree while memorizing her lesson plan in her mind. She will walk into a classroom of restless children and transform chaos into curiosity. Her calm will teach more than her textbooks ever can. Who would imagine the storms she hides beneath the calm?

There's a doctor tying her hair into a bun, her crisp saree neatly pinned, her phone already buzzing with patient calls. Her assistant sends her patient updates. She hasn't had breakfast yet, but she smiles as she rushes out - she knows that one reassuring word, one touch of empathy, can make someone's pain bearable, can cure someone, can give someone a ray of hope.

There's an entrepreneur, balancing invoices and recipes, her kitchen filled with the aroma of pickles and spices. Her hands are busy, but her mind is fierce. She knows profit and loss, but also the art of patience. Her business doesn't just sell - it gives her wings. She is quality check, manufacturing operation, finance, and marketing - all rolled into one person.

There's a mother waiting outside a school gate, a grandmother walking to the temple, a young woman boarding the metro with a laptop bag over one shoulder and a dream over the other. They all carry something - responsibility, ambition, love - but they carry it lightly, with grace.

And yes, there are struggles. There are moments when the saree feels heavy, when the pleats come undone, when the mirror reflects exhaustion instead of confidence. But even then, she straightens her back, smooths the fabric, and moves on with her head held high and her heart steady.

Because that's what Indian women do. They move on -not out of submission, but out of strength.

We have been taught to see power as something loud - to imagine it in boardrooms and battles, in voices that command attention. But in truth, power often lives in silence - in a woman who endures, who rebuilds, who keeps the rhythm of life going even when no one notices.

That quiet strength, the kind that smiles while it struggles, that nurtures while it fights, that forgives while it endures - that is the strength I wanted to write about.

I have always been vocal about women's rights. Society's dichotomy towards women has forever irked me. Our ever-evolving culture still holds a mirror to women - as mothers, wives, employees, leaders - and expects them to reflect grace, patience, and sacrifice. She is expected to manage it all. And she does - so beautifully, so silently. But why do we not talk about these women who do the extraordinary in ordinary circumstances?

This book is not just a collection of biographical journeys.

It's a mirror-one that reflects the unspoken power that generations of women have carried quietly on their shoulders. Sometimes showing quiet resilience and sometimes fierce determination but never ever giving up.

Some wear their strength like armour; others hide it beneath gentleness. Some build, some heal, some lead, some love- all of them leave the world a little stronger than they found it.

They are not extraordinary because they do everything.

They are extraordinary because they do it all and still smile.

Each woman in these pages represents a different shade of courage - bold, patient, fiery, or forgiving - but together, they form one image:

STRENGTH DRAPED IN A SAREE.

CHAPTER 1

WHY I CHOSE A SAREE?

When I first began writing these stories, I didn't set out to write about women. I set out to write about strength. The one that doesn't announce itself, doesn't need applause, doesn't even ask to be noticed. It's the strength that hums softly in the background of our everyday lives, the kind that gets up at dawn, wipes away tears before the world can see, ties back her hair, drapes her saree, and begins again.

The strength that is displayed by every woman, from the house help to the lady who comes to apply henna on our palms, from the manager at the bank to the teacher in a school.

That strength, calm, rooted, undemanding, became the soul of this book.

When I was searching for a title, Strength Draped in a Saree came to me almost instinctively. It felt like it had always existed - I had just finally found the words. The phrase, to me, is not only poetic but deeply personal. For me, each of the 10 women I have interviewed is like a pearl. What ties them together is a string.

The string is a Saree. Women, I have realized, may look delicate from the outside but are formed from resistance, layers, and time. You cannot crush a pearl easily. It shines because it has endured.

The Saree as a Symbol

A saree, for me, has never been just six yards of fabric. It's history that breathes. It's culture that adapts. It's identity that never apologizes.

When I see a woman drape a saree, I see an invisible ceremony take place - a moment of pride and self-possession. It doesn't matter whether it's starched cotton or soft silk, plain or embroidered - the saree carries a certain dignity that instantly transforms a woman's bearing. Her shoulders straighten, her walk changes, her presence deepens. She makes heads turn, she honours age old tradition, while keeping her modernity intact.

In India, the saree has been the witness to our most meaningful moments. We wear it when we want to feel rooted-On our graduation day, when we want to honour where we came from, On the day we receive an award, when pride sits quietly beside gratitude, at weddings, when joy flows through generations, at farewells, when memories cling like the folds of the fabric itself.

It is the attire that holds emotions, not just aesthetics.

But the saree has also evolved -just like the Indian woman.

It now walks into boardrooms, into airports, into television studios. It doesn't just belong to temples or festive days anymore; it belongs everywhere a woman chooses to stand tall and carry a legacy with her.

And that, to me, is the heart of the modern Indian woman - deeply rooted, yet limitlessly modern. She knows her worth, not because the world tells her so, but because she has seen what she's capable of surviving.

That realization first dawned on me as a little girl.

CHAPTER 2

STRENGTH DRAPED IN A SAREE: AMMA

As a young girl, I often watched women juggle their lives - balancing home, work, children, and everything in between. They moved like dancers in rhythm with life but following the dance routine already choreographed for them -one hand stirring a pot, the other holding a pen, their minds constantly split between what was and what must be done.

But there was one woman I can never forget. She wasn't family, she wasn't a friend- she was *Amma*.

Amma wasn't remarkable by the world's standards, yet she was unforgettable to me. She was the first woman who made me understand what quiet strength looks like -the kind that doesn't need to shout, the kind that simply endures.

When Amma Walked In

Amma would visit our house once every month. You could always tell it was her because she had her own music -the creak of the front gate, the shuffle of her black Kolhapuri chappals, and her voice, that soft Gujarati lilt calling out, "Didi, aayi gayi hu!" Didi, by the way, was my grandmother. As an Indian tradition, like all other women are to each other, didi, bhabhi, chachi, aunty- no one is a stranger.

My grandmother would immediately call her in. Amma would walk in with her wobbly gait -her silver hair oiled and tied into a neat bun, with few strands astray from the bus ride she had taken to our house, her cotton saree draped the Gujarati way. She carried a big black jhola with her, like an entrepreneur carries the weight of responsibility on her shoulder.

She'd place it down gently on the floor, almost reverently. She would start unpacking it like a magician revealing her treasures - theplas, jars of achar, farsan, papad, and of course, the sticky imli toffees that we children loved so much.

She would quietly hand one to us as my grandmother inspected the other items. They exploded like bombs in our mouths, the taste of Amma's hand autographed on each bite we took. The smell of roasted besan, turmeric, and hing would fill the house, mixing with the sound of her laughter and my grandmother's conversations with her.

The Stories inside the Bag

While the adults haggled, I'd sit quietly nearby, waiting for Amma's stories. She told them so simply - without drama, without self-pity - just like one talks about the weather. To her it was a simple conversation but to me it was a cinematic experience.

Her husband was bedridden, she said once. "He hasn't walked in years."

Her son and daughter-in-law had left home, taking her grandchildren with them. She spoke about them softly, never bitterly. Her eyes always gleamed with joy when she spoke of her grandchildren. She loved feeding them hand cooked meals. But the irony was that the hands that fed so many could rarely feed her very own kin.

Every morning at four, she would begin her day by kneading dough, mixing spices, packing orders, labelling jars and then, with her jhola full, she would leave for her rounds. She'd walk from one end of the neighbourhood to the other, her saree absorbing the sweat and dust of her daily battle for survival.

I remember being too young to understand hardship, but old enough to see her courage. Her face had lines of fatigue, but her eyes had light.

She didn't complain. She didn't blame. She just did.

The Bargaining and the Bond

My grandmother and Amma shared an unspoken friendship. They pretended to argue about prices, but both knew it was mostly for sport. Amma was a smart woman, I bet she bonded well with most women. But she never demeaned anyone. My grandmother would mockingly scold her.

"Amma, you always charge more!" my grandmother would complain.

And Amma, smiling, would reply, "Arrey Didi, you think I'm becoming rich from this?"

Both would laugh, both would argue, and both would finally agree - every single time. It was a ritual as comforting as the smell of her food.

When the transaction was over, Amma would pack everything carefully back into her jhola -always leaving us children a few imli toffees secretly. "Don't tell Didi, " she'd whisper conspiratorially.

Before she left, she would finish the tea and biscuits my grandmother had offered her, adjust her saree, sling her bag back on her shoulder, and smile. "Next month, I'll bring mango pickle, " she'd promise.

And then she'd walk away, her figure growing smaller as she disappeared down the lane.

I always stood by the window watching her leave. Something about her walk stayed with me - slow, tired, yet purposeful. There was a rhythm to it, like she carried music only she could hear.

The Lessons I Didn't Know I Was Learning

At that age, I didn't understand it, but Amma was teaching me something far more valuable than any lesson at school. She was teaching me what strength looks like when it's silent.

Years later, when I sat in a management class learning about manufacturing, operations, supply chain and finance Amma's face suddenly came to my mind. I smiled to myself.

She was every department rolled into one - the manufacturer, the quality control head, the packer and labeller, the salesperson, the delivery person, and the manager.

Her work began before sunrise and ended long after sunset, yet she carried it all with humility. She didn't have a business plan or investors. Her only capital was her hard work and her will.

I realized then that while many of us study leadership and entrepreneurship in schools and colleges, people like Amma live it-quietly, efficiently, and with extraordinary discipline.

The Woman Who Represented So Many Others

In hind sight, I know Amma was not alone. There are countless Ammas all around us if we choose to observe. They are the women who wake before dawn, who pack tiffin, balance accounts, care for families, and still find time to create something of their own. Some make pickles, some teach children, some run small businesses, some are henna artists, some are dancers and some just hold families together through sheer will.

They don't think of themselves as extraordinary, oh! but they are.

They are the heartbeat of this country - unseen, under-acknowledged, but unbreakable. They are the reason behind a smiling husband opening his tiffin to smells of spices each day, the reason why a struggling man never quits as he finds a stack of cash being handed over to him quietly during times of struggle, a reason why children go to school neatly with books in their bags and so many more.

Amma may have been one woman, but she symbolized millions. She carried the weight of her home, her pain, and her purpose, all in that one black bag.

The Full Circle

As the years passed and grand liberalization made manufacturing and scaling easier, people started believing that potato chips from packets and store-bought toffees were more "hygienic" options. Amma stopped visiting our home so often. It must have been her age too. Years passed. I grew up, got married, and life carried me into a new home with new roles. Amma became a memory-one of those faces you tuck away in a safe corner of your heart, certain you'll never see again.

And then, a few years ago, something happened that felt like life winking at me.

One afternoon, in my *sasural,* my in-laws' home- I saw a silhouette of a woman, same wobbly walk, same noise of the slippers, same Gujarati accent. "*Amma?*" I wondered. She carried a large, black jhola over her shoulder. Her silver hair was tied in a bun and she wore a similar cotton saree draped in the Gujarati style.

For a moment, time stood still. My heart jumped. Without thinking, I walked up to her and gently tapped her shoulder. "Amma?" I whispered.

She turned around slowly and though her face was older, her eyes had that same warmth, that same kindness. "Yes".

I smiled, almost laughing through tears. She wasn't the same Amma from my childhood, but in that instant, it didn't matter. She was Amma.

I invited her in, made her a cup of tea, and sat with her as she unpacked her jhola -filled with pickles, papads, and that familiar smell of asafoetida and mustard oil. My mother –in-law was "didi" now and I was still waiting for my imli toffee.

As she spoke about her life, about her children and her struggles, I found myself listening to her with the same awe that I had felt as a little girl years ago. Her words, her grace, her spirit it was as if time had folded back upon itself.

That day, sitting in my in-laws' home, I realized something powerful. Amma was not one woman. Amma was every woman every mother, every wife, every grandmother who carried her world in silence.

What Amma Taught Me

Amma taught me that work done with sincerity is never small. She taught me that grace doesn't come from wealth, but from dignity. And she taught me that strength doesn't always roar -sometimes, it just gets up at 4 a.m. and starts kneading dough.

Even now, whenever life feels heavy, I think of Amma. I imagine her waking before dawn, her kitchen smelling of oil and spice, the sound of the stove crackling as the first batch of theplas browns on the tawa. I can almost see her standing there, tying her saree tighter, and adjusting her jhola, ready to step out again.

Whenever I think of Amma now, I don't see her as a figure from my past. I see her as a symbol of endurance, grace and womanhood that bends but never breaks. And maybe, somewhere out there, she still walks through quiet lanes with her black jhola, her steps steady, her heart full, carrying not just food but hope - one home at a time.

Because women like her never really leave. They live on in our stories, in our memories, and in every quiet act of courage that keeps the world moving.

She was and will always be, Strength Draped in a Saree.

CHAPTER 3

PERSEVERANCE DRAPED IN A SAREE: OLYMPIAN PARAMJEET CHOUDHARY

"If we do not try everything is impossible, but if we try everything is possible"

Paramjeet Choudhary was born in Meerut and brought up in Bikaner. She is a former Indian athlete with many feathers to her cap. Her glorious contribution to the nation comes from her gold medal in the 4*400m relay at the 2000 **Asian Athletics Championship in Jakarta**, as well as medals at **the South Asian Games and other international meets**. She also represented India at the **Sydney Olympics in the year 2000**, where her relay team created history by breaking a long standing national record.

For her unparalled achievements, she was honored with the **Maharana Pratap Award, Aravali Award, and Nahar Sanman Puruskar**. In her, more than a decade long athletic career as a track specialist, she has shown valor, grit and diligence towards the nation and the sport that became her life. Not letting the shine of her medals fade, **she continued to serve the nation by choosing public services** as her next step. Now she serves as an officer in the Indian Revenue Service, becoming the first woman Olympian in this service. Her journey reflects not only strength, but a calm ease with which she turned challenges into milestones.

From Television to Tracks

As a child Paramjeet had no inkling that one day she would make the nation proud.One evening, she sat before the television, wide eyed as the Seoul Olympics of 1988 were being telecast. **On the screen flashed some of World's finest athletes- Ben Jonson and Carl Lewis, their strides like those of a panther, their spirits unshaken**. To her, they became idols instantly as she saw them move at lightning speed to conquer the tracks.

For Paramjeet, it all seemed so simple. "**If they can run, so can I**", she thought to herself innocently. When the athletes marked their positions on the track, ever observant, Paramjeet noticed the spikes on their shoes. She turned to her father Mr. M.S. Bindra, a government serviceman in Bikaner, and asked him for "**shoes with nails**"; not knowing that athletes call them spiked shoes or running shoes. On the eve of her birthday, to her utter astonishment, a pair of shining spiked shoes awaited her.

They looked more like wings to her dream, ready to lift her to the same world she had witnessed on television.

With those shoes on, she ran with all her might, imagining herself alongside Ben Jonson and Carl Lewis. But reality was harsh. She fell, scraped her knees several times. But she didn't give up. With each bruise her resolve deepened, she knew she needed practice with precision, guidance and technique. So this time she went and asked her father, not for another pair of shoes, but for something greater- a coach.

Seeing her zeal, her father arranged for one in Bikaner itself. **Coach Satpal Singh became her guide, her mentor- the Krishna to her Arjun**. Under his discipline and vision, Paramjeet's raw enthusiasm for racing was forged into skill and perseverance. And thus began the long and determined journey of a girl who dared to follow in the footsteps of world's sprinting legends.

Stepping into International Sports

It was her spirit and her sprint that led her to the 2000 Olympics. Paramjeet remembers that their training was no less than what they show in movies- the same sweat, same grit and same visceral almost sacred feeling, that she was doing something for the nation. She stepped onto the international sporting arena as early as 1992, competing in the 4*400m relay at the Singapore Open Track and Field Championship, **where her team won Gold**.

But that medal didn't satiate her. **She believes that without hunger, one cannot achieve anything.** As she strode along this path through the yearly schedule of competitions, from Asian

Athletics Championships to National games, all Paramjeet saw was that one empty shelf at her home which she could fill with another trophy. Every sprint she took was with more courage and more determination towards the ultimate goal- to make India proud at the Olympics. Not only did Paramjeet win on the field, but her discipline and mental strength helped her excel academically as well, proving how physical training can strengthen mental well-being.

Breaking Shackles along with Records

It was the year 2000. The Inter State Senior Athletics Championship was being held at Chennai. The Women's 4*400m relay team consisting of Paramjeet Kaur (Starter), K.M. Beenamol (Finisher), Jincy Philip and Manjima Kuriakose stunned everyone with their performance. Not really considered strong contenders, **they shocked everyone by breaking a thirteen year old National Record**. A record of 3:31.55 seconds set by none other than P.T. Usha and her team at Rome in 1987**. Their timing was a smashing 3:28.11 seconds.** For Paramjeet the moment was no less than shock and with pride combined together. That evening she called back home, fumbling and crying at the same time, telling to her parents that SHE WAS GOING TO THE OLYMPICS.

At the Asian Athletics Championship held at Jakarta, Indonesia, later in the year 2000 the Indian 400m * 4 relay team shattered several records again. **This time they brought the Gold home, beating Japan and South Korea**. For Paramjeet, the moment of standing on the podium, listening to the National

Anthem play as the tricolor went up, was nothing short of life itself- a culmination of years of sweat, sacrifice and unshakable discipline. That victory was more than a medal; it was a declaration that **Indian women runners could carry forward the torch lit by legends like P.T. Usha and shine with pride on the Asian stage**.

The Starter of Dreams

In the build up to the Sydney Olympics in 2000, Paramjeet faced a setback that could have shaken her confidence. While some teammates were sent abroad for training she had to stay back and continue training, on home soil. **Instead of seeing it as a loss, she treated it as a test of her resilience.** Her coach advised her to aim for the sixth athlete's position, since 6 players were being considered for the relay squad at that time. But Paramjeet told herself, "All this hard work just to be the sixth athlete, a bench player? No**, I WILL be a starter**." With that inner resolve, she trained harder than ever, sometimes vomiting on track, sometimes facing physical exhaustion but never giving up. She told herself, "Paramjeet, this is the one time you have to give it your all, then life is awaiting with all the accolades you dreamt of."

That perseverance soon bore fruit. Earlier that year in Jakarta, she had already made her mark at the Asian Athletics Championship, and when she finally wore India's colors at the Sydney Olympics, it was proof **that if one believes in themselves and enjoys what they do, there is no holding back**. Not only did Paramjeet make it to the team, she in fact was the STARTER. Their team broke another National Record at Sydney.

STARTER is a suitable definition of Paramjeet. On track, she was the starter in India's 4*400 m relay team, the one who set the pace, carried the baton forward, and gave her team the thrust to dream. **Off the track, she was once again a STARTER- the first Woman Olympian to join the Indian Revenue Service, breaking new ground in civil services** just as she had on the field. For Paramjeet being a STARTER was not just about taking the first lap; it was about opening doors, setting examples, and proving that with discipline and determination, one could begin new journeys in sports, in academics, and in public services.

Reflective message to Young Athletes

Paramjeet often reflects on how different the sporting world looks today. "Now there are tracks everywhere and so many facilities, " she says, "In our times, we measured the roads with our feet and practiced laps on rough stretches, because proper tracks weren't easily available. **We trained with what we had – grit and determination were our equipment.** Yet out of those modest times, Champions were made.

To the young athletes of today she offers a message born out of struggles and triumph; "It is not easy – **athletics demands immense physical and mental strength**. But then tell me, what comes easy in life?" she asks rhetorically. She speaks for all of us when she says that, every field, whether you are a man or woman, will test you. **What matters is that you remain focused, disciplined, and determined**. Enjoy what you do at every step. Not everything will be smooth, you may fail, you may fall sick, you may stumble. But on the track, or whatever arena you choose, you should aim to be a trailblazer." She acknowledges the fact that it is the small battles we fight daily that make us win the war.

The Disciplined Motherhood

Beyond the track and beyond office, Paramjeet **found her truest role in motherhood**. She took complete responsibility for her children. She managed everything on her own, balancing the demands of her family and professional life with quiet strength.

For Paramjeet discipline and good health have always been the foundation of life. She **recalls her father waiting by the tracks during training days, after his office hours**. Once she was home from practice he would prepare health shakes and juices for her recovery. This lesson, she has passed on to her children too. Even while she travelled abroad, she never indulged her children with chocolates. She taught them that the **strength of mind begins with the strength of body**. Today her children stand as a reflection of her own belief-grounded, healthy and driven. Her son represented India in the World University Games in Germany, recently, making India proud just like his mother.

Equality is achieved through Determination

On being asked about competing in, what many call the "man's world", Paramjeet Choudhary is clear and fearless in her reply. "Why should we even consider ourselves weaker?" she asks. "**Men too have struggles. We, as women, are equally strong if not more**; we endure labor pain, almost equal to breaking many bones in our body." As an athlete and as a high ranking officer, she believes that women limit themselves only when they accept that they are weaker. But the truth, she feels, is different. "**We can do it all**, " she believes, "manage homes, take care of our children, succeed at work, and excel in our own fields. Nothing should be seen as a burden. We must keep moving forward."

The Advice to the Homemakers

To the women who have immersed themselves in family life, she has one advice**, to take out two hours a day for themselves.** Not to rest or relax but pursue a hobby, to pursue good health. "Every day find time to exercise, if you have time, jog, just walk at home, exercise a bit, eat healthy, give your children healthy homemade meals as much as possible. With a little bit of discipline, we can achieve a lot."

She believes that physically strong women are mentally strong too. And such women definitely raise wonderful families. Families that together achieve success and fulfill goals, stand up for each other.

Paramjeet Choudhary's life is a reflection of strength shaped by discipline and love. As a daughter, she carried forward her father's belief that hard work builds body and character. As an athlete, she turned that belief into Gold for the country. As a mother she passed the same value to her children. Her story reminds us that true champions are not born but created with quiet determination and perseverance. *Perseverance draped in a Saree.*

CHAPTER 4

WISDOM DRAPED IN A SAREE: EDUCATIONIST RUPKATHA SARKAR

> *"Nothing can compare to the psychological salary of a teacher. It is the love and respect they get."*

Mrs. Rupkatha Sarkar stands as a radiant figure in the Indian Education diaspora. As the Lady Principal of the prestigious institution, La Martniere for Girls, Kolkata, she has guided generations of students with a blend of intellect, compassion, and vision.

In a career spanning more than thirty years, she has been honored with **Swami Vivekananda Award from the International Human Rights Council** and the **Mother**

Teresa International Award for Education, recognizing her commitment to holistic teaching. More recently, she was conferred the **Beacon of Excellence Award – 2025 by IIHM**, acknowledging her exemplary contribution to education. Her journey is one of respect, honor, and touching lives with her discernment.

Childhood Influenced by Teachers

Ever since her early childhood, Rupkatha knew she wanted to be a teacher. **For as long as she remembers, the classroom was her dream**, so much so that she recreated it at home. She would wear her mother's stoles as a saree and create a small desk for herself just like she had observed at school. She would emulate her teachers, her walls and doors filled with chalk writings. She would conduct her own make-believe classes with great seriousness.

As a young student at the reputed St. Thomas Girls School she was fascinated by her primary teacher Miss Young. Her indulgence and her kind compassion tugged at Rupkatha's heart, sowing the seeds of a lifelong passion. It is only now that she realizes the efforts Miss Young put in to shape many lives like hers.

As Rupkatha grew, she was **lucky to always find teachers who were inspiring as well as compassionate**. They instilled discipline in her and an urge to serve society through her erudition. Her senior school biology teacher with her crisp saree, graceful aura, and lucid style of teaching, became her true idol. The lessons went beyond textbooks, leaving a lasting impression-one that still reflects in Rupkatha's teaching style today.

Perhaps her dream was also in her blood- her mother had always wanted to be a teacher, but due to family responsibilities she couldn't pursue it. She never let her daughter face the same adversity. **The seamless transition of aspiration from a mother to her daughter was always supported by her parents.**

Educated to Educate

Rupkatha came from an affluent family where teachers' pay parity compared to other professions in those times, did not dissuade her from following this virtuous path. Armed with a Graduate Degree in Botany from the prestigious Presidency College, a Post Graduate degree from Calcutta University and a Bachelor's of Education Degree from St. Xavier's College, her academic diligence and grit helped her transition into the role of a teacher effortlessly.

One of the early lessons Mrs. Sarkar learnt as a teacher **was that she was allowed to be human**. Once, while teaching a class, in a hurry to complete the syllabus before the examination she taught one chapter less. The students were aware of this and requested her to give one chapter less for the examination. It struck a chord with her, making her realize that it is alright to create an organic student to teacher relationship, with mutual respect for one another. This taught her that students are a teacher's best judge. "**Students can see beyond the façade**" she says. "**Over a period of time they can differentiate between style and substance**". Hence, she believes that **teachers, who teach students lessons of life, counsel them and help them**

grow as human beings, are the ones the students will never forget.

Even after her marriage and children she was able to steer away all apprehensions about this dream. "Teaching", she said, "has always been an extension of my personality. It is an indispensable part of my soul and my identity"

Being a mother: A Child's First Teacher

As a mother she was always present for her children, even though many times she had question papers to correct, lessons to plan and a lot more. From a very early age she explained to her children that her profession was demanding but they were her strength. She always let her children become independent human beings both in thought and work. Her children grew up in discipline, not restrictions.

She asserts that for the first few formative years of a child, a mother's presence is paramount. But **with adequate family support, a mother can manage both her career and her home**. The elderly ladies of the home must support and hold hands of the younger generation. The elders should use their authority positively.

"For the growth of a child", she says, "A wholesome and happy environment is more important than everyone being present around the child all the time". This she affirms, by stating that, many times, working mothers raise more independent and self-reliant children. Not discounting the efforts of housewife, who she thinks are the foundation of homes, she would still like to see more mothers going back to their careers post motherhood.

Finding Our True Purpose

"**We all have a purpose in life**", she says, "**Given the talents we have as women, as people, we must use them for the betterment of the society**". She believes that families also benefit from the career of a woman. She has observed a paradigm shift in this area, over the years, as a teacher, as a Principal and as a counselor too. Yet she feels there is a gap. Women, sometimes more educated than their partners, have to sit back and take family responsibilities as they do not have adequate support.

Empowerment for the women, she believes, is in the mind and not the external trappings. Modernity, according to her, does not lie in clothing, lifestyle or indulgence, but in how one uses their freedom to benefit others around them, bring a change, to the society and foster a meaningful environment.

A Teacher is the Greatest Gift to the Human Mind

The message Mrs. Sarkar has for today's aspiring teachers is equally profound. According to her, teaching and mentoring is a calling of the heart and the noblest of professions. **It offers stability, dignity, and a rare gift of influencing lives in the deepest way**. Though the salary may have limits, the true reward lies in the "**psychological salary**"-the love and gratitude that no other profession can equal. Very vocally she asserts the fact that,

"To us teachers students are a batch, to that ONE student, it is that ONE teacher teaching him or her"

She observes that **teachers also need to reinvent their anecdotes, their stories and their teaching pedagogy to stay relevant**, as in today's fast paced world the role of a teacher is ever evolving. Sometimes she is like a mother, nurturing the children, sometimes like a counselor and sometimes imparting lessons, just like a teacher. She believes that students are now asking questions without inhibitions. And as teachers she states. "We must have the answers."

Nurturing the Future

She upholds that all her students-now spread globally in diverse positions- **were nurtured by her with her Head, Heart and Hands**. Through an analogy she describes how she feels when she meets these students- she says, "We sow seeds as teachers, we don't even know how big this tree will grow, what fruits it will bear." It is like a surprise gift to her every time she comes across a student she has taught in the past. She affirms it is her duty to impart them with adequate knowledge to face the world. **Her students are her protégés not prototypes**. She mirthfully recalls meeting her students at events where they remind her of how she reprimanded them for their mistakes. But the very next moment they, themselves justify, that this is how their future was shaped.

The Journey of Wisdom

Mrs. Sarkar's journey stands as a testament to what it truly means to be an educator. Even after all **the awards and accolades-which**

she regards as society's kind gesture to acknowledge her work- she holds that her true calling remains in teaching, in constantly reinventing herself, and in discovering new ways to shape young minds. **For her teaching is a higher purpose, one that changes the society bit by bit**.

She concludes by expressing gratitude to the countless **teachers in remote areas who, despite harsh circumstances and without expecting anything in return,** dedicate themselves wholly to their students' betterment. To her, that **selfless devotion represents the richest and purest form of education**. In her we see not just a teacher, but a wife, a mother, a daughter, a daughter-in-law and so many other roles that a woman is given. Those that she carries with quiet grace, never allowing them to overshadow her devotion in the classroom. For her students she will always be the epitome of wisdom. *Wisdom draped in a Saree.*

CHAPTER 5

RESILIENCE DRAPED IN A SAREE: DR. ARUNA TANTIA, ILS HOSPITALS

> *"As a mother it is never easy to be anything else first, but with support and shared responsibility we can make it work."*

Dr. Aruna Tantia is a shining example of a woman standing at the intersection of science and humanity. She carries an aura of quiet strength that only healers possess. As the Director and Consultant Gynecologist at the renowned and prestigious ILS Hospitals she has been more than just a doctor in a white coat- she has been a beacon of hope and health for many women. As the founding member of the ILS Hospital she has been a part of the hospital's growth and management, taking it to greater heights.

Her journey is decorated with honours, but each award tells a deeper story of service. When the world shut down during the pandemic, she chose to step forward. For this courage, **the Government of Tripura conferred upon her the Chikitsa Ratna Samman, recognising her unwavering dedication during COVID-19**.

Her excellence in the field of women's health and surgical innovation earned her a place in **India's Best Doctor Awards as the Most Profound Gynae Endoscopic & Reproductive Surgeon in Eastern India**-a title that reflects decades of commitment, precision, and empathy.

Her leadership extends beyond the operating room. **Rotary International District 3291 honoured her with the Star Committee Chair Award for her outstanding contribution** in the field of medicine as well as her philanthropic endeavours. It is a testament to the impact she creates in the community as a whole. And under her guidance, ILS Hospitals has flourished, receiving the Eastern India Leadership Award, Bengal Excellence Award, and ABP Ananda Swastha Samman, mirroring the vision she brings to the institution.

Early Seeds of her Calling

Being born in an affluent business family, Aruna grew up in an environment where ambitions, goals and enterprise were part of her daily life. Her mother, an impressive business woman in her own right, became her first role model. She instilled in her **the importance of self-belief and independence.** Young Aruna simultaneously found an inspiration in her uncle, a practicing doctor in the UK. His balance of professional success as well as harmonious family life left a lasting impression on Aruna's mind. While she noticed that business families often struggled to take out time for their families, she admired how doctors with their structured routines, could nurture both careers and families. Her brilliant academic record in school, along with her fearless, adventurous spirit unafraid to challenge norms, laid the foundation for her calling.

The Determination of Carving a Path

As the eldest among three sisters, Aruna carried the weight of societal expectations but her non-conformist attitude helped her carve a path of her own. In the 1980s when medicine was still considered a profession "suitable" for men, Aruna was ready to give it her all. Her journey however was not one without stumbles. Under Jaipur's rules, she was required to study one year in college before joining medical. She couldn't clear her Pre Medical Test at the first go, an early set back that tested her resolve. Her mother, though initially reluctant to see her pursue medicine, changed her mind when she saw the fierce determination in Aruna's eyes: **the unmistakable spark of someone determined to make a difference.** It was then that her mother told her, "If you want to become a doctor you have to marry your career first. There is no looking back from here."

Initially Aruna had dreamt of joining the Armed Forces Medical College, for which she prepared by enrolling for Air NCC cadet. She trained by learning riffle shooting and flying light power air crafts. Though the sky was her first ambition her dreams were winged in another direction. **She joined the prestigious RNT Medical College in Udaipur under Rajasthan University. Later she obtained her MS in Obstetrics & Gynecology from Mata Gujri Memorial Medical College.** It was during her final year in medical college, where destiny introduced her to Dr. Om Tantia, her future husband, through a family arrangement. Even before their marriage, a confluence of individual dreams was shared. As if destiny had brought them together for a greater cause, the dream of building a hospital of their own. This common ambition became the foundation of their life long partnership.

Shaping her Career: From on State to Another

The real struggle of pivotal choices began when she moved to Kolkata, then Calcutta, with her husband to take care of their family as well as work, together on a mission to serve the society. At that time Bengal had rigid domicile rules in medical education. Only those with at least eight years of connection to the state were eligible for post-graduation medical training. For an "outsider" opportunities were scarce. Instead of letting this policy limit her ambitions, **Dr. Aruna reshaped her path, choosing gynecology**, a field that not only matched her skills but also aligned seamlessly with her husband's surgical expertise.

Then came the challenging decisions of her life. Shortly after the birth of her first child Dr. Aruna was offered a Laparoscopy fellowship at the prestigious Northwick Park Hospital, UK. Accepting it meant leaving her infant behind, enduring long separations, relying on sparse trunk calls, entrusting her mother in law with her new born. Though she was confident he would be taken care of, her heart wrenched at the thought of leaving her child behind. But for the greater good, for the sake of the oath of service she took when she became a doctor Aruna did what most others couldn't think of in those times. It was a monumental sacrifice.

Breaking Stigmas and Bringing a Change

After the fellowship Dr. Om Tantia and Dr. Aruna Tantia started practicing at the prestigious Anandlok Hospital, where Dr. Aruna dealt with stigmas of patients towards keyhole surgery. One incident left a deep mark. A female patient was discouraged by another senior doctor for a Laparoscopic Hysterectomy, where she discharged herself before the operation. This showed the struggle they had to face **as pioneers of a technology still nascent in Bengal**. It wasn't just the procedures of the medical field they had to deal with but the years old dogmas and the aversion towards the ever evolving medical practices they were bringing to the table. It wasn't easy to break these shackles that even some of their own field's professionals weren't readily accepting, leave alone the patients.

But their dedication, their willingness to endure personal hardships and their shared unwavering faith took them to a new journey. They worked day and night, convinced people through practicing and preaching both. And of course with their impeccable capabilities as well as successful surgeries they were able to create history in Eastern India. Their names were associated with pioneering and path breaking work. Their popularity grew.

The Birth of ILS Hospitals

In the year 2000, under the vision of Dr. Om Tantia, and the guidance of Dr. Aruna Tantia, the foundation of ILS Hospitals was established with the help of supportive colleagues. The unending encouragement of family and their own determination turned ILS into the Healthcare Institution it is today. A success story built on struggles, self-motivation, self-belief, and an undying commitment to bring the best of their capabilities to the forefront.

Dr. Aruna always believed in supporting her fellow doctors as well as new entrants to build this legacy. With expansion to other cities like Agartala, Dr. Aruna found herself oscillating between cities for training new members, her home and the existing hospital which was expanding too. Brick by brick, bed by bed and with the faith of patients pinned on them; ILS grew into a trusted Institution.

Motherhood: the Act of Balancing

Yet, amidst the demands of medicine and management, Dr. Aruna was always focused on her role as a mother. From very early on in their careers, she and Dr. Tantia had divided their responsibilities carefully. She would leave for the hospital only after her children had left for school in the morning, and she would be back before them— ensuring she was home when they returned. In an era without mobile phones, she taught her children the landline numbers of every medical facility where she could be reached. **They memorized them by heart, a lifeline of connection in her absence**.

Dr. Aruna recalls the delicate balancing act of those years. If one parent sacrificed evening hospital shifts, the other took the onus of being present for major events or parent teacher meetings at school. They celebrated their children as much as their careers if not more.

"**As a mother**, " she reflects, "**it is never easy to be anything else first. But with support and shared responsibility, we made it work**." For her, family life was not a tradeoff but a parallel priority.

Her philosophy is simple yet profound, "We can make up for some of the lost time later in life. But in each moment, we must give a hundred percent of ourselves to whatever we do."After delivering over 2000 babies and with an experience with new mothers as well as women of various diaspora **she offers two guiding principles**:

1. Switch off from all other roles when you are with your children whether you are a working mother or not. Whatever time you dedicate to them, even if it is an hour it should be theirs.
2. Master the art of time management and schedules

As a gynecologist she emphasizes the **importance of a mother's presence during the formative years of a child**. Yet she believes that with adequate support –whether in a joint family or nuclear- a woman can achieve anything. "Too many women, " she cautions young doctors, "miss out on family life in their race with male colleagues. Do not hitch yourself to the top in a hurry. Excelling takes time and patience."

A True Philanthropist

Today, with her children grown and well-settled, Dr, Aruna devotes her Sundays to causes close to her heart. She conducts women's menstrual health awareness campaigns through the Matri Raksha Project for over 20, 000 women, promotes girls' education in villages, and organizes medical camps for rural communities. She is a member of many causes through Rotary International. "Limbs are provided to the limbless" through the Mahavir Seva Sadan. For her**, philanthropy is not a duty but peace**, "the joy of giving to people you may never see again, knowing they cannot give you anything in return, is blissful." She says with a smile only women with great experiences and greater determination can say.

The Medical Legacy

Dr. Aruna Tantia's story is a shining example of how resilience, grit, and determination enable a woman to stand **tall in her profession without compromising her family life.** She has shown that it is possible to balance both worlds -nurturing her family while building a medical legacy- and emerge as a true inspiration for generations to come.

With her grace and grit, with her heart in the right place and her mind at the right pace Dr. Aruna Tantia is not just a name but a force in the Medical field, one that will be etched in history for future generations of Doctors and Women. It will teach them that women are like rivers carving new paths every day tprovide water where growth, prosperity and nurturing is required. She is truly Resilience Draped in a Saree.

CHAPTER 6

NATURE DRAPED IN A SAREE: DR. KABERI KAR GUPTA, ECOLOGIST

> *"Before anyone else we need to preserve nature for ourselves, for our future existence."*

Dr. Kaberi Kar Gupta stands as a visionary environmental scientist and a wildlife biologist whose soul is attuned to the whispers of the wild. Her pioneering research on the Slender Loris in Tamil Nadu opened new paths in conservation science, while her fearless investigation into the illegal turtle trade network exposed the hidden wounds of nature in the early 1990s. **Founder of the Urban Slender Loris Project and recipient of the Paul Shin Award for the Unsung Heroes of Science Education and**

Communication (2019), she entwines science and empathy with rare grace. Scholar storyteller, a conserver of nature, guardian of the unseen, Dr. Kaberi Kar Gupta truly blends intellect with intuition and reason with reverence.

Nurtured by Nature

Kaberi grew up in Khardah, West Bengal, with her parents- both school teachers and devoted nature lovers, and her aunt. Their roots were in rural East Bengal, now Bangladesh-an area filled with flora and fauna. **They built a home surrounded by farmland and forest patches, replicating their native surroundings, smoothly converting their respect for nature to their aspect of living.**

The area was an industrial suburb of Kolkata back then. **But her house stood like a green sanctuary, alive with the rustle of leaves and the distant hum of the Hooghly River**. Her parents gave her the freedom to wander barefoot through fields, watch insects, and listen to whispers of the wild. Her aunt, who cared for her as a child, never stopped her from muddying her feet. She doesn't recall the need to ever visit a Wild Life Sanctuary or a Nature's Park as a child. Botany echoed in her surroundings.

Nature versus "Development"

As Kaberi entered her teenage years, the world she loved began to fade- the trees were felled, the farmlands shrunk as more housing was required for the increasing population. **The birds and jackals were replaced by bustling city folks**. The call of birds was replaced by sirens of workers call. The loss stirred a quiet storm in her heart. She rebelled against destruction, unable to accept nature's erasure. In her heart she knew how important it was to channelize her anger into determination. It was important to find a cause to be associated with.

Luckily for her Khardah had a diaspora of Science Clubs which allowed her to experiment with Nature's choicest blessings. She participated in many events to create awareness and gain exposure. With this foundation, she moved on to study Zoology in college. Science clubs made her interested in science, especially biology.

A Life Changing Mentor

Kaberi pursued Zoology for her Bachelor's Degree. **It was during this time that she met her mentor and guiding force, Dr. Pankaj Manna, a devoted naturalist and a scientist** who opened her eyes to the wild beauty of forests. From field trips to villages to connecting with the tribal folks of the deep forests of Jharkhand, through NGO work under the guidance of Dr. Manna, she felt an unshakeable pull towards the wilderness- it was where her heart truly belonged.

One day she chanced upon an ad for the Master in Science Program at the Wildlife Institute of India, Dehradun, in Employment News- a weekly newspaper. It interested her. Encouraged by Dr. Manna and her parents, who put their foot down for her, in front of other elders of the family, Kaberi applied for the entrance examination. She was determined to give heed to her calling of the wild. Her father accompanied her to her maiden trip to Dehradun, **where she earned her place and a scholarship from the Ministry of Environment and Forests.**

Life at the Wildlife Institute of India

However the transition was not easy- the fieldwork was demanding with lots of study material- but Kaberi embraced every challenge.It was very different pedagogy in comparison to other science fields- one where being in tandem with nature was sanctimonious. **From researching the common Langur to studying birds in Arunachal Pradesh,** from **pioneering the Slender Loris Research Project to researching turtles threatened by poaching in Bihar, to working as a field biologist in Kalakad-Mundathurai Tiger Reserve**, she found purpose in struggle. Each field work reaffirmed what she had always known - her soul belonged to the wild.

Kaberi married her senior from the Wildlife Institute of India, **Dr. Madhusudan Katti, an ecologist whose fascination with the ecology of birds (Avian Ecology) mirrored her own love for the wild**. Their primary dedication was towards nature. Dr. Madhusudan went first to the University of California. It was here that he followed the flight paths of migratory birds around the continent. He went back to the University every year as the migrant warblers went to their wintering grounds, while she would delve deeper into forests for her field work, giving them very little time together.It was much later that Kaberi went to the USA too, to the Arizona State University.

Foraying into the Wild

When Kaberi Kar Gupta first started studying the slender loris in the forests of Kalakad-Mundanthurai Tiger Reserve, **she didn't imagine it would take her months to find the very creature she had come to study - the Slender Loris.** "It took me more than a month, maybe two, to see the first one, " she says, smiling at the memory. Each night, she and her small team of field assistants would walk through narrow trails, torches flickering in the dark, unsure if they were even looking in the right direction. "We had to figure out everything ourselves. You can't study them the way you study other animals." **Even a senior scientist who joined her once went back without seeing a single loris.** Still, Kaberi didn't give up. Then one night, two tiny eyes shone back at her from the branches above. In that quiet moment, patience turned into discovery -and the journey that began there became India's first long-term behavioural study of the Slender Loris.

The forest, though, had its own tests waiting for her. Kaberi worked with a team of five - four assistants and herself - and danger often came without warning. Elephants and bears would appear from nowhere; forcing them to run for safety and abandon the field work for that particular night. **"You learn to be alert every second, "** she says. But the harder part wasn't just surviving the wild; it was navigating a world of men who didn't always see her as an equal. "You have to be careful -not just of the wild animals, but of people too, " she admits. It is here that she felt that in a male-dominated field, women are challenged and work more to prove that they are as capable as their male counterparts. Putting on make-up would be considered girlish. Even though during menstruation woman were allowed to rest, they wouldn't like to lag behind in their research and would work doubly hard once they were back in the forests. **It wasn't the villagers who thought women couldn't be in the forest but the urbanites.**

Motherhood and the Forests

During her Ph. D in the U.S.A, Kaberi decided to have her first child. Motherhood reshaped her life and changed her perspective towards life. "Before that, everything was planned, " she recalls. "**I knew exactly what I wanted to do-finish my research, get back to the field in six months, and continue my work with my team. But life, and childbirth, had other plans**." Unexpected health complications after delivery delayed her work by over a year, testing both her resolve and patience.

Living in the U.S. at the time, she and her husband managed everything on their own. "We had a very supportive network of friends within the university, " she says. "That made all the difference. We'd take turns watching each other's children so one of us could work." Despite the challenges, Kaberi balanced it all with quiet strength.

When her first child turned one, she came to India with her off spring in her arms, returning to the forests, the field, and her research, this time not just as a scientist, but as a mother who had learned that **nurturing life and researching primates were two sides of the same calling**. In the Mundantharai Reserve she found support in the form of villagers and locals who knew her from her earlier days of studies and field works she had done there.

Her sister or her parents visited her sometimes to take care of her child. Studying the Slender Lorises which are essentially nocturnal animals meant she would have to adapt her child's sleep schedules to her research work. The local indigenous communities helped her.

Kaberi had picked up the Tamil language and befriended the villagers and this helped her find safety and nurture for her child even deep in the forests. "The villagers were like family, " she says fondly. "**They took care of my little girl when I was out in the field. They'd keep her safe; feed her, play with her, while I spent long hours tracking the animal.**" Their kindness touched her deeply. In those dense forests, far from home, Kaberi found care instead of isolation-a village that embraced both the scientist and the mother in her. While others questioned her decision, for Kaberi it was instinctive, nature had always been her safest home. **Inspired by pioneers like Jane Goodall, who had taken her own child into the wild, Kaberi believed that raising a child amidst nature was not reckless but restorative**. It was, to her, the most natural way to nurture strength, curiosity, and compassion, the very lessons the forest had once taught her.

From Forest to University

When Kaberi returned to the U.S., life brought a different kind of challenge. Her first child had just started preschool, and she was still trying to finish her dissertation when her second baby arrived. "I took up a full-time teaching job when my younger one was only five weeks old, " she says, shaking her head at the memory. Recovering from a C-section while teaching, researching, and caring for two young children was far from easy. **With no day care available, she began carrying her baby to class in a small sling. "Sometimes the students thought it was just my bag, " she laughs.** It was exhausting, but she carried on teaching with quiet strength, proving that determination isn't only found in the wild. Sometimes, it lives in a mother standing at a blackboard, doing it all, one day at a time.

Instilling the Love for Nature

She believes that parents should allow their child to be closer to nature and teach them primarily to respect nature. From the small crickets that surround the house, to the little bird that stops by our window everything is a part of a bigger ecological system that deserves validation and conservation. **She feels that more the people are walking away from nature, the more mentally stressed they are getting.** "Even in these big urban jungles try to make your children aware of nature through visit to parks, small field trips and sightseeing at farm lands, " is the only advice she wants to give to mothers. "Life doesn't happen in isolation, " she says, "as a mother we are nurturers just like nature itself." She asserts we must make our children more aware of nature's gifts.

She doesn't believe in being pseudo nature lovers. **She believes that for adults it is a responsibility to preserve nature for the future generations to come.** Just a visit in jeep to sanctuary or a visit to a resort where you look at nature from air conditioned rooms is not enough to create awareness. "Pick up that piece of garbage, protest cutting down of trees, lead an ecologically friendly life" is her appeal to all.

Empowering and Imparting Knowledge

Today, Dr. Kaberi Kar Gupta continues to live a life intertwined with nature, even while teaching and mentoring in the United States. **As her children were too young Kaberi switched to work in urban ecology and consulting while she was in California's Central Valley**. She now serves as a Research Associate at the North Carolina Museum of Natural Sciences, where she contributes to biodiversity and conservation research, and as a museum advisor and educator, guiding young scientists to see nature not just as data, but as connection. **Through her collaborations and lectures, she continues to remind people that science and compassion must coexist**.

Having lived lives that juxtaposed each other Kaberi is an exemplary woman with grit and grace both. **Every few years, she returns to Khardah, to the sound of rain, the scent of soil, and the trees that first taught her to love nature**. Her journey began here. But now with the excessive pollution and increased population she reminiscence her old home, where she still lives in spirit. She marks, "Our house in the USA is surrounded by urban forests. It does not look like you are living in an urban area. We live in a house surrounded by wildlife and large trees", exactly how she wanted her Khardah home to be preserved. For Kaberi, the forest is not just a place; it is home. She is, truly, *Nature Draped in a Saree.*

CHAPTER 7

COMPASSION DRAPED IN A SAREE: MRS. REKHA SHARMA, SOCIAL ACTIVIST

> *"Feed your family but also feed another family if you can. Celebrate your festivals but also wipe someone's tears"*

Mrs Rekha Sharma stands out as a woman who believes that compassion and inclusion form the foundation of real progress. **As the Chairperson of the East Zone-CSR at CCI Logistics Ltd., she has dedicated herself to giving corporate social responsibility a heart** - one that beats for the marginalized and unheard voices of society.

At CCI Logistics, Rekha has transformed CSR from a formal obligation into a movement of empathy. Her vision goes beyond symbolic gestures; it is about creating spaces of dignity and belonging. She believes that true empowerment begins when every individual, regardless of gender, background, or identity, is treated with respect. **Her exemplary work for the transgender community for over one and a half decade has not only created an awareness towards the community but has also given them a voice- one which had been silenced in the by lanes of Kolkata for the longest time.**

Legacy of Good Deeds

Rekha did not come from hardship. She was born into an affluent and respected family in Dhanbad, raised in the coal-lined lanes of Jharia, a town where life was raw, voices were loud, values were simple, and character spoke louder than wealth. **The greatest influence in her life was her Dadaji, a man who held no formal position yet commanded extraordinary respect.** People came to him with disputes. He listened before he spoke. He stood with wisdom rather than judgment.

"**He had *rutba*- not from status, but from integrity**, " Rekha often says when she speaks of him. In that courtyard where villagers gathered and her Dadaji mediated lives with compassion and firmness, Rekha absorbed her first lesson-leadership is not declared, it is earned through service.

She went on to study at Balika Vidya Mandir in Jharia and later graduated from SSLNT Mahila Mahavidyalaya in Dhanbad.

In her community, education for girls was encouraged, but only as a prelude to the real expectation-marriage.

Marriage and a Little More

Like every young woman around her, Rekha stepped into marriage with grace and obedience. She moved into a prominent joint business family-a world of structure, routine and unsaid rules. As one of the younger daughters-in-law, she carried the silent weight of responsibility. The rhythm of her life was defined by family duties. **She never complained; service came naturally to her**.

After eight years of marriage and a quiet wait for motherhood, Rekha was finally blessed with two sons and a daughter. **Life became fuller, louder, and beautifully chaotic. Between school tiffin, family rituals and the endless responsibilities her days were full**. But Rekha was not a woman who let life define her; she shaped it with her own strength. Independence was not a choice for her, it was her nature.

Even as she drove her children to school, managed a home and balanced family expectations, she continued to step out for what she believed in. She wanted her children to grow not just with comfort but with courage. **"Dream beyond boundaries, "** she would often tell them. And she meant it. With her encouragement and determination, her children now pursue higher education- even cities and crossing countries. When they flew out to build their own futures, Rekha did not step back-she stepped forward. With her children studying away from home, she now had the time to deepen her commitment to society.

It was her husband, Mr Satish Sharma, who encouraged the voice of compassion in her. **He had seen in her something rare, not generosity, but empathy**. He watched her connect with people others ignored like the daily wage worker, the house help cast aside after years of service, children of labourers who carried hunger in their eyes. "You were not made for a small life, Rekha, " he once told her, not with dramatic persuasion, but with quiet conviction. "Your heart was built to serve. Don't hold it back."

Turning a New Leaf for a Greater Cause

With his encouragement, **Rekha stepped beyond the walls of tradition-not in defiance, but in purpose.** She began working with the CSR division of their family business, and what started as a simple step into social work slowly became a spiritual mission. Life was no longer just about roles, it was about responsibility. Service gave her breath. And purpose gave her movement.

What she didn't know then was that destiny was preparing her for a community-not to rescue them, but to stand beside them as they reclaimed their dignity. Rekha was about to meet the transgender community, and nothing about her life would ever remain the same.

Recognising and Reckoning the Force

Rekha began her journey to help the transgender years ago. **She was intrigued by the Divine strength the transgender held-a strength that helped them survive as the other side of a society for centuries.** What started as a quiet effort of support and inclusion slowly grew into a social awakening in Kolkata, an awakening powerful enough to move the administration, media, politicians, corporate leaders and ordinary citizens. She still remembers the very first-time she started the event. It was chaotic yet peace giving and it changed something inside her.

For nearly two decades now, she has led special pre-Durga Puja homage for the transgender community, not as a CSR formality, but as a celebration of existence. She gave them visibility with respect.

In 2024, her initiative under CCI Logistics carried the theme, **"Embracing Inclusivity - 600 Voices, One Heart." Six hundred members of the transgender community gathered-not as invitees, but as honoured guests**. Their seats were in the front row, their names were announced, and their stories were heard. No one asked them to sing or dance for entertainment. They were not treated as symbols of superstition. They were celebrated as human beings.

Speaking to the press that day, Rekha said gently but firmly, "**They have always been a part of our society. We are not giving them a place-we are acknowledging the place that was always theirs**."

Her words carried truth, and truth travels. The media covered her, not as a corporate CSR face, but as a woman who dared to stand beside those that the society had kept outside its gates.

Spreading Good Deeds

By 2025, her movement had grown into a tradition Kolkata began to recognise with pride. Local coverage described her annual gathering as "One Heart, 600 Voices – A Celebration of Belonging." For the 19th consecutive year, Rekha stood tall, not on a stage, but with the people she serves.

That year, something remarkable happened: power came to witness compassion.

Political leaders joined her-not because they were invited, but because they believed in her work. MLAs stood on stage beside her. Young Political Leaders attended, adding a voice of support. Respected social workers came forward not as guests, but as allies in the movement.

This was no ordinary program. It was a mirror to society- a reminder that inclusion is not a speech-it is an action.

From the dais, Rekha spoke with emotion in her voice. "**The strength of Maa Durga lives in every soul that survives rejection and still chooses to live with courage. This community has that divine strength**." And the crowd stood silent—not out of formality, but out of respect.

Empowering Women

Her circle of compassion widened. Along with her work for the transgender community, she began working for women in distress **through her NGO, Nari Sashaktikaran Sangrah**. She stood beside women who had been silenced by fear, those facing violence behind closed doors, those rising from emotional and financial abuse, those trying to rebuild their lives piece by piece. She did not just hear their stories, she stood with them through their storms.

During the pandemic, she witnessed a side of society that broke her heart in a way she could never forget. One day, the officer in charge of a police station called her for urgent help. Outside the station sat a group of women who weretired, hungry, and forgotten. **These women came from vulnerable parts of the city, from lives where survival itself was a daily fight**. With nowhere to go and no work because of lockdown, they had been without food for days.

"That day, " Rekha recalls softly, "I saw the two faces of society more clearly than ever before. One side was safely locked inside disinfected homes, washing vegetables in fear. The other side was sitting on empty stomachs, not worried about infection butjust fighting to stay alive."

She reached out to people she knew, asking for support to distribute food. Only a handful turned up. But that did not stop her. **When kindness became scarce, Rekha's determination only grew stronger.** She vowed that no one in her reach would ever go to sleep in hunger again.

From that moment in 2020, Nari Sashaktikaran Sangrah was born as a movement of responsibility. **It did not begin in an office room; it began on the streets, in hunger, in helplessness, and in the unwavering belief that compassion must be practiced, not preached.**

Rekha often says that while serving the underprivileged is important, sensitising the privileged is equally necessary. Social work, she believes, cannot survive on sympathy alone-it needs hands, hearts, and collective effort. "If someone can contribute money, let them. If someone can volunteer time, let them. If someone can offer skills or physical effort-*shram daan*-let them, " she says. "Every hand that joins makes the chain of humanity stronger."

To build this spirit of shared responsibility, she began organising small gatherings of women she knew-friends, professionals, homemakers, entrepreneurs-inviting them not just for events, but for purpose. But she also noticed a harsh truth about society:

"Most people want to celebrate-but not many want to serve, " she observes.

She has seen it too many times. **During Navratri, people line up little girls, worship them as Kanya Devi, touch their feet, offer them food-and the very next day, pull up their car windows when another child comes begging at a signal.** On Gopashtami, many donate fodder to cows-but the rest of the year, they walk past hungry animals without a thought. Festivals move people-but consistency changes lives.

Rekha speaks of this with disarming honesty. "If a new café opens in the city and I invite forty women, thirty-five will happily turn up. But if I say-come, let's feed abandoned animals in an ashram or distribute food to the hungry-maybe ten will come."

She doesn't complain-she persists. This is because her mission is not to gather crowds. It is to awaken conscience.

Her life is proof that a woman can take care of her family and still serve society. She says, "Do good, not once a year but every day, in every small way you can."

She has taught this to her children-not through words but by example. Compassion is the legacy she has chosen to pass on.

Indifference versus Involvement

In a world where indifference has become normal, Rekha chooses involvement. Where people choose silence, she chooses voice. Where most look away, she steps forward. **She has the courage to call leaders, officers, institutions-and even society itself-to action. And she does it not with aggression, but with grace. That is her power.**

Rekha Sharma is not just a woman who works for society-she is a force who moves it- soft heart, strong spine, and fearless purpose. She is *Compassion Draped in a Saree.*

CHAPTER 8

EMPATHY DRAPED IN A SAREE: ANAMIKA GHOSE, CHILD COUNSELOR & CHAMPION FOR SPECIAL NEEDS

> *"Find your own tribe and if you don't find them, then build one and if you can't build one, continue to stay authentic"*

Every child is a story waiting to be heard, and Ms. Anamika Ghose has devoted her life listening to those silent stories. **A seasoned child counselor Anamika has dedicated over 18**

years of her life to schools like The British School, New Delhi, Pathways World School, Aravalli, Gurgaon, The Doon School, Dehradun, St. Thomas Day School, Kolkata and the oral School for Deaf Children.

For her commitment to her work with students she has been the recipient of many awards. She received the prestigious Telegraph Award in the year 2000. In the year 2020 during Covid, she was awarded the **Exemplary Educator during Unprecedented Times Award by the Centre of Assessments for Excellence**. She also **received the Dr. Radhakrishnan Award in the year 2023 for her outstanding contribution to the field of education**. Her belief that every child deserves a fair chance in education despite their unique abilities has made her a beacon in the field of education and counseling.

With a career rooted in empathy and inclusion, she began as teacher in Kolkata, nurturing young minds. It is here she realized the need to champion the cause of Special Needs and Wellbeing. Her work reflects deep commitment to creating supportive spaces for students with diverse emotional and learning needs. **What society and most schools shy away from is exactly what Anamika has embraced- nurturing children who see the world differently.**

Roots of Empathy

Born in Kolkata, Anamika began her education at Loreto House School. **Her parents planted the seed of social dedication in her heart.** She learnt that she had a responsibility towards society from examples rather than theory. Her father was a doctor by profession and an altruist at heart, who served at the free clinic that was supported by the Alumni of the St. Xavier's College in Kolkata. Her mother, a passionate educationist herself, while she served as the Junior School head at St James'School, Kolkata dedicated her time to the Ekta Evening School for underprivileged children. Anamika started teaching craft and dance to less fortunate students through the "Each One Teach One" initiative. Witnessing her parents' compassion, especially her father's belief that "Your Karma is Your Dharma" deeply influenced her. Empathy ran through her blood.

The Turning Point

A defining moment for Anamika was when she saw her neighbors' child Zubin living with cerebral palsy. He lived in social isolation. Often finding it difficult to do what most kids could easily manage. She saw the pain in his parents' eyes and the daily struggle to bring up the child without proper guidance and counseling. **This wrenched her heart into supporting people with special needs.** Though she dreamt of becoming a doctor, her tryst with science was tough. But with her purpose in place and determination in her heart, she still found a way to care for the children she connected with through teaching, counseling and social services.

Anamika's journey into service and developing a love for the world of psychology began at a very early age at Loreto House, where she imbibed the lessons of empathy, integrity and service-**learning to do the right thing even when no one was watching and putting service before self.** Later, at Pratt Memorial School, her leadership roles in Nature Club and Interact Club gave her a sense of purpose, leadership and the confidence to turn compassion into action.

As she grew her desire to study psychology at the reputed Fergusson College, Pune met initial resistance from her paternal grandfather. He felt that she could pursue her career in Kolkata and stay safe at home. Yet it was her father's quiet conviction and her grand **Aunt Muriel Singh's unshakeable support that became her pillars.** Aunt Muriel, a wise and steadfast teacher, often reminded her that education was a woman's greatest strength. With their blessings, Anamika stepped beyond her comfort zone to chase her dreams.

Truly Nurturing her Calling

Life in Pune was liberating yet demanding. In a class of twenty five students with two boys, she realized that psychology was seen as "soft" subject- but to her it was discipline of depth, empathy and strength.

After her Masters in Applied Clinical Psychology from Calcutta University, **her compassion took her to newer avenues like the Oral School for Deaf Children.** She was holding hands of those whom the world turned away for being different. It was Jeru Postwala, this School's Principal who told her, "You have a gift Anamika, use it well." Encouraged she trained as a teacher, blending her knowledge of psychology with her heart for children. She was guided by mentors like Mrs. Ayesha Das, who was a legendary educationist, who always told her "Be a teacher by choice and not by chance and that is what makes a teacher a shaper of good and kind human beings for the future world."

The Quest to Conquer Hearts

One of her first clients in her professional journey that began in Kolkata was a stressed mother who came to her in tears stating that her child was being threatened to leave school as he couldn't cope academically. The hurdle she faced during the treatment after realizing the child had ADHD was not just to make the child feel safe, but to make the father believe that it was a condition and not a disease. **The child went on to conquer most educational barriers with great zeal.** He saw Anamika as a "Story Aunty", as she used social stories to guide him. With this incident she realized the alarming need for acceptance of Neuro Divergent students in schools and tragically at homes. She, however, worked with them as they were-children who see the world a little more uniquely than others.

In due course of time Anamika worked with many Institutions and students. To each of them she was a Healer. While she was in Gurgaon she faced one of the biggest challenges of her career: a student of great potential and dreams to be a physicist one day but hindered by a barrier-blindness. The child was proof that dreaming didn't require vision but dedication**. She along with the Institute head, showed unwavering faith and displayed tireless efforts to help the student**. She collaborated with teachers and the IBO to ensure the student was provided the access to learning and accommodations required for a student with visual impairment. Although she left the school before he could graduate in the IBDP program, she felt that her small contribution to a boy with such courage and determination graduated and is gone on to pursue a College degree in computer science

During her two years at The British School in Delhi, Anamika met a young student who faced significant learning challenges. The daunting challenge was that the student may not be able to work with the curriculum and that his academic levels were not at par. But **Anamika saw something others had missed-a spark, a will to try, and a heart full of kindness**. With her belief that *"if you can dream it, you can do it,"* she began working closely with the child and his parents, who shared her hope and unwavering faith. **They became a team, celebrating every small victory and learning to see progress not in grades but in courage.** Through patience, creativity, and constant encouragement as well as a leading team of dedicated special educators, Anamika helped the child find his own rhythm of learning. Today, that same child continues his academic journey, now in Grade 10, pursuing his IGCSE-an inspiring reminder of what faith, compassion, and perseverance can achieve when a teacher truly believes in her student.

Another example of her act of silent heroism was the mentoring of her student Shabeeha Ahmed. When Anamika started teaching psychology Shabeeha was one of her first students. **Not realizing her true potential Shabeeha had almost given up hope of making it big in life**. But Anamika supported her and mentored her as a true teacher would. Shabeeha now gives Anamika hope, as she is a teacher herself. Shabeeha too mentors all her students as own. Just like she was once nurtured by her teacher Anamika.

She was not just a teacher to these students, but somebody who sculpted a path for them to follow. If all teachers became like Anamika the word disability and students lost in ambiguity would truly disappear.

Embracing Motherhood

On the personal front Anamika was ready to take on the responsibility of having a family. Though being with children was her calling, she yearned to have her own child. **Motherhood at forty didn't seem to be delayed, but one filled with prior experiences and learning from all the mothers she worked with.** Yet it is a unique experience to her. Now as her daughter Isa is growing she feels that her personal growth and career trajectory have slowed down but has never stopped. As a woman who works, she believes that she can create a good understanding of the real world for her child. As a professional, having her own child has made her even more empathetic towards mothers and their journeys with their children.

Effect of Changing Family Dynamics on a Child

She asserts that the shift to nuclear families, the support of a grandparent is indispensible. To her they bring assistance, but to a child they bring a whole era to the table. The line is blurred as she cares for her mother and her mother cradles her child. This unique bond she believes is where the roots of Indian families lie in this age and time.

Parenthood, however, according her is a shared goal as well as shared responsibility. Putting the onus of a child on the child bearer alone is a long gone thought. **She believes a father's role is to provide equal amount of time and dedication in a child's growth, without judgments**. Children are more aware of their parents' roles now. As she observes through many of the cases she has dealt with. It was not just mother who was involved but the father too. This is the basis of the new age home according to Anamika.

For Parents of children with special needs she advises not to use search engines as their psychologist**. She urges them and teachers to remember every time the child is "discussed" or a solution is asked for the child loses a bit of himself or herself.** Acceptance, she believes, is the first step. The second step is to allow a professional to guide them. With consistent measures and patience, parents can positively reinforce a children's belief in themselves. She believes that celebrating small goals of the child, creating realistic milestones and giving time to their child can help them live a life of peace and joy.

Technology is a Boon if Dealt with Sensitively

She believes that technology plays a major role in parenthood these days. With advent of newer avenues in the field, the awareness towards special issues in children has increased. Anamika believes it is easier to convince parents and schools alike to hone the talents of those who are Neurodivergent. Parents understand and believe in Anamika's reassurance towards the betterment of their child.

For Anamika technology, in terms of children's use, is not an enemy but a gift- one that must be handled with care and consciousness. She asserts that children learn balance when adults lead with trust and example**. Instead of a stigma towards screens, she urges parents and teachers to guide their use with love, consistency and clear boundaries.** For example: For educational purpose the parents should encourage children by teaching them the use of creating power point presentations or word documents, in real life. Children learn better when they are treated with respect more than restrictions. Mindful use of technology does not require control but inculcation of wisdom to choose right.

From one Woman to Another

To women she advises to be authentic and not to compare themselves to others. **"Find your own tribe and if you don't find them, then build one and if you can't build one, continue to stay authentic**, " she says, "It's alright be standing alone, what matters is you keep believing in yourself."

"Staying grateful for what you have on your plate, what you have in your days and what you have physically is the biggest strength." She says with a compassionate glint in her eyes.

To mothers she has a very potent message:

1. Your children are a reflection of your actions, choices and beliefs so always stay true and are mindful of what you choose to be.
2. Accept that your child is your gift, priceless and non-returnable - make the most of what you have. It is your gift and your responsibility to care for it no matter what shape, ability or kind.

Creating a Pedagogy through Compassion

Anamika Ghose's journey is one of quiet strength and boundless compassion. Through her work she has not only guided children but also helped parents rediscover the joy of understanding and connection. **Her belief that every child is unique and every emotion valid reflects a heart that listens before it speaks.** In a world often quick to judge, she chooses empathy as her compass-reaching out, reshaping minds, healing hearts along the way. She stands as true embodiment of grace and understanding- *Empathy Draped in a Saree.*

CHAPTER 9

AESTHETICS DRAPED IN A SAREE: MRS. MANJARI SAHAI, INTERIOR DESIGNER

> *"The word 'impossible' is not in my dictionary.*
> *Even with my clients, I tell them - it will be done.*
> *And then I learn how to do it."*

For nearly four decades, **Manjari Sahai has been a name spoken with quiet reverence in the world of interior design**. Through her firm, Enhance Designers, she has crafted homes, offices, restaurants, and hotels that echo not only her sense of aesthetics but also her belief in balance, dignity, and soul.

What began out of curiosity and passion in a modest corner of Calcutta grew into one of Bengal's most respected design practices - built not on marketing or visibility, but on integrity, instinct, and an unrelenting pursuit of excellence.

In 2025, when her daughter Pooja Sahai Narsinghani received the Times Design Ikons East Award for Timeless Elegance in Classic Luxury Design, it was not just recognition of a company - it was a reflection of four decades of devotion, perseverance, and quiet triumph. "That award, " Manjari smiled, "wasn't just for design. It was for endurance, for faith - for staying true."

Roots That Defined Her Compass

Born in Jamshedpur, the eldest daughter of a respected Marwari business family, **Manjari's early years were a tapestry woven with discipline, values, and freedom.** Her grandfather, a deeply principled man, believed in tradition, culture, and order. Her grandmother, on the other hand, was a woman with less formal education but with thoughts far ahead of her times. She was remarkably liberal-warm and independent-minded.

Together, they raised her with a balance of roots and wings. Her grandmother, though uneducated, believed fiercely that girls must have a voice and a choice. Religion was never enforced, food was never restricted, and curiosity was never curbed. "She gave us space to question, to express, to exist as we were, " Manjari recalls. "That was rare in those days."

Her father, an industrialist, filled her world with the sounds of construction -hammers, chisels, and the hum of creativity. Her mother, soft-spoken yet progressive, taught her that strength can be tender, and modernity can sit beautifully beside tradition. "From her life, " Manjari says, "I learned that gentleness doesn't mean weakness, and conviction doesn't mean defiance." It was her family that taught her to think deeply, observe closely, and never take beauty at face value.

A Child Who Saw Life through Lines and Light

Even as a young girl, Manjari was drawn to the rhythm of building and making. She would stand beside carpenters, watching how wood obeyed the human hand, how precision and patience gave form to imagination.

"While other children played outside, " she laughs, "I was happiest standing near the workers, asking them why they cut a beam this way or that."

During festive visits to industrial bungalows in Jamshedpur, she absorbed proportions, geometry, and the relationship between space and comfort. "Even as a child, I never saw a house as just walls and furniture, " she says. "To me, a house was alive - it held the stories of its people."

That perspective-that spaces have souls-would later define her design philosophy.

A Love Chosen with Conviction

In her final year of school, she met a man who would later become her husband - thoughtful, older, and deeply respectful of her individuality. Their bond grew slowly, built on trust and conversation.

When marriage was proposed, it met with resistance. Her grandfather worried that her fiancé's modest income would not sustain her lifestyle. But Manjari was unwavering. "You must choose a person for who he is, not for what he earns, " she told her family.

The quiet Arya Samaj ceremony that followed was more than a wedding; it was a declaration - of independence, equality, and the belief in love over luxury.

That same courage - the willingness to step away from convention yet carry her values with grace - would later echo in every choice she made.

Every Home, A Beautiful Canvas

Marriage took her across cities and homes - thirteen in total. For most, shifting homes repeatedly is exhausting; for Manjari, it was exhilarating. Each move became a blank canvas, each new space an opportunity to reimagine warmth.

"I used to get excited, " she smiles. "Every wall spoke to me. I'd paint, rearrange, design - it was my joy."

Friends began noticing. They admired how she turned bare apartments into living, breathing homes. They sought her advice, first casually, then professionally. "I didn't realize it then, " she says, "but I was already living my calling."

A New City, A New Beginning

The family's eventual move to Calcutta was unplanned. They had prepared to relocate to England and had already given away most of their belongings. "We came here with nothing - three daughters, no furniture, just courage, " she recalls, with a half-smile that carries both pride and nostalgia.

Those early Calcutta years were difficult - a rented home, rising expenses, and endless domestic responsibilities. But in her, the quiet fire of ambition had begun to burn. Her mother's voice echoed in her heart -"You have so much talent. Why are you wasting it?"

It was around this time that Mr. Modi, a family friend from the Hindustan Development group, recognized her innate design sensibility. Encouraged by him, she decided to take the leap into professional design.

Through Mr. Modi, she met Mr. Adhikari, a self-taught architect whose business had recently failed. When he offered to work for her, she astonished him by suggesting a partnership instead. "You have the technical experience, I have the vision, " she told him. "Let's build something new."

Together, they started with nothing but conviction.

From Scratch - With Courage as Capital

Manjari began working from her father's office on Park Street, Calcutta's prestigious business district. It was symbolic-a young woman with no formal training sitting every day at a desk, waiting for work that wouldn't come.

For six months, there were no clients, no phone calls. Her father, though supportive, worried But she stayed. "He didn't doubt me because I was a woman, " she reflected later. "He doubted me because he saw me struggling - and he couldn't bear to see me fail."

To bridge the gap between instinct and execution, she joined British Paints (now Berger Paints). Within a month, she learned drafting, layouts, and technical drawings. "If you don't know something, " she says, "you can either wait or learn. I chose to learn." Even while at British paint she would always try to achieve the aesthetics and designs that others felt were impossible. Even some of her teachers were impressed by her ability to grasp concepts and mould the impossible into possible.

Her first big project - a residence on Camac Street - arrived soon after. She remembers the long nights, meetings stretching past eleven, walking alone to find a bus home. "I didn't even know where the buses stopped, " she laughs. "But business teaches you -patience, humility, and fearlessness." **She could have easily asked her father or husband for their cars but to her professionalism was top priority**. She saw independence as a boon and a bane. A boon that made her ambitions successful and a bane that made her self-reliant even in the toughest of situations.

Setbacks and Survival

Just as her career was finding momentum, life took another sharp turn. Her husband's business collapsed, leaving them with ₹500 in the bank. **It was a test of endurance- financial, emotional, and spiritual.** Though circumstances were not conducive, Manjari always had the knack for looking at the problem in the eye. Not one to give up Manajri continued with hard work and dedication.

Her husband rebuilt slowly, travelling abroad to find new opportunities, while she held the fort- raising the children, managing the home, and sustaining her young business.

She used her first project's advance both to pay suppliers and to run her household. **Her honesty became her identity. She was a natural at managing her finance.** It was magic, even in hard times, she never defaulted with creditors, managed her home, supported her husband, all at the same time. "When you come from a business family, " she says, "you learn that your word is your biggest asset."

This integrity became her foundation - and soon, her reputation. People would visit her on-going projects, word of mouth had started spreading sealing her golden reputation in the interior designing business. Projects began coming in - first from Hindustan Development Corporation, then Tega India, and gradually, from some of Calcutta's most influential names.

The Workshop of Dreams

Her small workshop became a cradle of craftsmanship. She found artisans who could translate her vision into form. "There was one carpenter, " she smiles, "who could understand my ideas just through gestures. I'd move my hands like this -and he'd sketch exactly what I saw."

Piece by piece, they created furniture that carried character. Her designs weren't just about grandeur -they were about warmth, proportion, and harmony. And Manjari, she absorbed it all with the same childlike glee, she showed at her father's sight of work.

"Spaces must breathe, " she explains. "A home should comfort you when you walk in. It should hold your chaos gently."

The journey, however, was far from smooth. She faced financial setbacks, clients who defaulted, and even harassment, which she handled with quiet dignity, walking away when her principles were crossed. **What kept her going were her daughters.** She wanted them to have choices, to grow up free and fearless. She gave them the same freedom she had been given - the freedom to think, to learn and to choose their own lives.

In all of this Manjari is grateful to her husband to let her have her choices, her career and her independence, something that was rare in those times. She speaks of her husband's quiet support with warmth. "He never expected me to follow all his traditions blindly, and he was always there for the children. That balance gave me strength."

The Invisible Support System

Manjari often credits her strength to the circle of women around her who helped her shape her career, by giving the wings of support to her dreams-her mother, who made her realise her dreams, her close friends who saw and spoke of her talents, her daughters, who are as fearless and determined as her if not more, and one unsung pillar: her housekeeper.

She ponders, "Often we forget to thank the people who have helped us most closely". For her the house helps were like family and that is exactly how they treated her daughters when she was away for work.

This acknowledgement - of another woman's role in her success -defines her humility and her understanding of shared strength. "We women rise higher when we lift one another, " she adds softly.

A Woman's Perspective on the Present

Now, at seventy-three, with decades of experience behind her, Manjari's reflections on womanhood are both profound and practical.

"Women today have more freedom, yes, " she says, "but they also have far more pressure. Earlier, our boundaries were defined - at least you knew where your responsibilities began and ended. **Now, those boundaries are blurred, and the world expects you to be everywhere, all the time -at work, at home, at social events, online.**" According to her woman today are being hailed as "Superwoman". But the question is do they really need the tag?

Advice for the New Generation

For young designers, her words are filled with wisdom forged in experience.

"There is always room for more designers, " she says, "but you must have passion- not the kind that burns out, but the kind that sustains you quietly for years."

She emphasizes that creativity alone is not enough. "Design has to have soul. If a project doesn't have soul, it shows. You can fill a room with the most expensive materials, but if there's no emotion, no intention, it feels hollow." For her, design is not about spectacle but about creating spaces that breathe and belong.

She encourages young women to treat clients with empathy, not ego. "Listen more than you speak. A designer's job is not to impose beauty, but to reveal it."

Her advice to women in any field is equally inspiring:

"Balance is not about doing everything; it is about realising what matters most today. Some days, your work needs you; some days, your child does. Either way, you're not failing -you're living."

A Legacy of Aesthetic Grace

After over forty years of shaping dreams into structures, Manjari Sahai remains an emblem of perseverance and purpose. **Her creations -from intimate homes to elegant offices and celebrated restaurants -are not just interior spaces; they are emotional landscapes.**

There are women who design homes, and there are women who design lives.

Manjari Sahai has done both -and done them beautifully. **Over the decades, she has shaped not just spaces, but souls, balancing family, work, and self with the kind of poise that comes only from inner strength.**

"I never believed in separating work and life, " she says with a quiet smile. "Both feed each other. When your home is happy, your work reflects it. When your work inspires you, your home glows differently."

That harmony became her art form. **She turned challenges into lessons, mistakes into stepping stones, and ordinary days into memories of meaning**. Her greatest reward, however, lies not in the awards or acclaim, but in the life she sees unfolding before her - in her children who have grown into grounded, accomplished individuals, each carrying a part of her essence forward.

Her legacy, quite literally, continues through her daughter Pooja Sahai Narsinghani, who has inherited her eye for design and her instinct for balance. Together, they've created a lineage of aesthetics - where modernity meets soul and creativity carries conscience. "When I see my children doing well, " Manjari says softly, "that's where my peace comes from. That's when I feel I've done something right."

She designs not for the eye, but for the heart. "When a client tells me they feel peace in their home, " she says, "that's my award."

Even now, at seventy-three, she enters every space with the same gleam in her eyes-curious, calm, and alive. "Age doesn't slow you down, " she says. "Losing passion does. And I've never lost mine."

With her blend of intuition, elegance, empathy, and endurance, Manjari Sahai remains, and will always be, a woman who built not just spaces, but stories and lived them with unshakable grace- Aesthetics Draped in a Saree.

CHAPTER 10

NURTURER DRAPED IN A SAREE: SREEMATHY VENKATRAMAN, CLINICAL NUTRITIONIST, ENTREPRENEUR & ADVOCATE FOR THE "FOOD IS MEDICINE" CONCEPT

| *"YOU ARE ENOUGH"* |

Sreemathy Venkatraman is a clinical nutritionist, therapeutic diet specialist and **the founder Mitha Aahara-** a visionary nutrition consultancy that weaves together ancient wisdom and modern science to heal through food. With over two decades of experience across multi-specialty hospitals, nutritional clinics and

ICU, she has dedicated her life to transforming how people think about food.

Her philosophy-*Eat to live, not live to eat*-speaks directly to today's fast-paced, convenience-driven generation. Over the years, she has guided thousands toward sustainable health, prevention and disease management using a blend of empathy, science, and cultural nutrition.

Sreemathy has received numerous accolades for her path breaking work. Most recently she has made India proud in Dubai, where she won the **MOST ICONIC WOMEN OF THE YEAR IN NUTRITION & DIETETICS-2025** at the Global Conference and Awards for Excellence & Leadership in Healthcare.

In addition, she received **the Excellence & Leadership in Healthcare Award as Bangalore's *Most Trusted Online Nutrition Consultant* at the Golden Aim Awards**. Her deep work in dysphagia won her the prestigious **Michael Donovan Award for Advocacy Leadership in Dysphagia**, honouring her contribution to supporting individuals with swallowing disorders.

Featured in many magazines and news channels, both regional and National, *including The Times of India, NDTV, Sun TV, and* more, Sreemathy continues to stand firm in her belief that food is not merely fuel—it is healing, heritage, and hope. As a speaker at many conferences, both national and international, she champions metabolic health and mindful eating. But long before the world recognised her expertise, she was simply a young girl with a dream much larger than her circumstances.

Childhood: Simple Living High Thinking

Born into a modest Tamil family in Chennai, the youngest of seven siblings, Sreemathy grew up in a home where resources were limited, but values were abundant. Her father, a government employee, and her mother, a homemaker, raised their children with integrity and quiet strength.

There were no household helpers, no luxuries-but there was warmth, prayer, tradition, and the aroma of fresh food that filled their home every day. From her mother, she learned one of life's greatest truths:

True strength does not raise its voice; it rises through resilience.

She excelled in academics with hard work. Her earliest lessons about food were not from textbooks, but from watching her mother cook simple meals with deep intention. She learned early that food could nourish more than the body-it could heal. With that conviction, she chose Home Science along with science in school.

Her First Inspiration: A Mother's Quiet Strength

Through every stage of life, her mother remained her source of emotional grounding. "For mental strength, my mother is everything, " she says. "I stand where I am because she stood for me."

When Sreemathy completed her graduation, she faced a crossroads no child ever wants to encounter. Her mother had just undergone stomach surgery, and at the same time, Sreemathy was selected for a rare Post-Graduate Diploma in Hospital Dietetics in collaboration with a U.S.-based university-an opportunity that included an internship at Christian Medical College, Vellore. Her family expected her to stay back. As the youngest daughter, it was "her duty."

Torn between duty and dreams, guilt began to weigh on her.

And then her mother said the words that changed her life:

"You will not stop your studies because of me. You will go."

Even in her illness, her mother fought for her daughter's future. That unwavering support became the foundation of Sreemathy's strength. She put Sreemathy before herself. Her mother proved to be her backbone.

Learning through Experience

Sreemathy honoured her mother's decision. She excelled in her course and went on to intern at CMC Vellore. After completing her postgraduate training, she worked across hospitals in South India, only to realise that nutrition in India was viewed differently then, restricted to illness and crisis.

"Back then in the early 1990s, hardly anyone understood what a dietitian actually did, " she recalls.

Her early career involved working with NGOs, neurology centres, and clinical departments, but she kept her purpose clear: to bring everyday nutrition to everyday people.

Purpose Meets Passion

In the late '90s, at a time when many were chasing dreams abroad, she moved to the United States after marriage. Her husband, an IT professional, became her pillar of support-encouraging her to continue her work in nutrition rather than abandon it.

She completed her Master's degree in Diet, Health & Disease, but later chose to pause her career for motherhood-a conscious, empowered decision.

"There are phases in a woman's life, " she says. "A pause is not a weakness. It is about prioritising what matters."

Motherhood: A Season of Grace

In a foreign land without extended family, she juggled motherhood and academics with quiet determination-studying during day care hours, writing research papers beside baby bottles, preparing for exams while gently rocking her child to sleep. Her life was filled with multitasking. But she was a determined woman.

Looking back, she says:

"I took a break, and at that time I felt guilty. But today I know—I chose right."

Her message to women is simple yet powerful.

"Do not feel guilty for taking a sabbatical. It is just a pause, not a full stop."

Caring across Distance

Living abroad taught her a new dimension of caregiving.

"Distance no longer means neglect, " she says. "Technology has bridged oceans."

From video calls to virtual medical reminders, she believes today's children support their parents differently, but no less lovingly.

Return home with a Purpose

After sixteen years, she returned to India and stepped back into her profession with sharper clarity and deeper compassion. What made her popular wasn't just her expertise it was her ability to speak science in the language of emotion and culture.

She learned different regional languages effortlessly and used communication as a bridge. She didn't just give diet plans she reconnected people with their roots, their food memories, and their identity.

Her upbringing had instilled a deep sense of self-reliance. Inspired by her middle-class culture and upbringing, she knew that opportunity was something you created, not waited for.

Her philosophy became her mantra:

"You are enough."

Not because you must do everything alone, but because true strength begins when you stop doubting yourself. "Ask for help when needed, " she says, "but never depend on it. Build yourself first then build your world." Her journey is not just one of success; it is a tribute to resilience. A reminder that dreams are not denied by difficulty they are denied by doubt.

Founding Mitha Aahara: Eat to Live

The idea of Mitha Aahara did not begin as a business plan. It began as a feeling that kept returning to Sreemathy through the years. Whether she lived in India or in the United States, one truth kept coming back to her.

"People heal best when they eat the food they grew up with."

During the pandemic, this feeling became a calling. People were scared and wanted guidance that felt scientific but also warm. **They wanted to cook familiar meals but did not know how to make them healthier**. Sitting at her dining table with nothing but her laptop, knowledge, and compassion, she created *Mitha Aahara -Eat to Live.*

There was no big office. No marketing team, just empathy, science, and courage.

Clients began reaching her from across time zones, each wanting help that honoured their cultural food. By understanding their "food DNA, " she helped them return to health through regional meals.

Word spread organically-not through advertising, but through trust. **That was the moment she knew that Mitha Aahara was not just a nutrition practice. It was a place where**

people could return to themselves. It was food as comfort, food as science, and food as identity.

The Science of Food: The Best Cure

For Sreemathy Venkatraman, food is more than nourishment-it is an identity, culture, and connection. "When I talk to someone in their mother tongue, " she says, "they often say, 'Oh my God, she understands me!' What they really mean is I understand their food."

India's diversity inspires her approach to nutrition. **"Our strength lies in our diversity-our cuisines, our languages, our traditions, "** she explains. Even festivals like Navratri, though celebrated across India for nine days, hold different meanings in every region. "I learn so much from my clients, whether it's how they fast for Navratri, Lent, or Ramzan, each practice reflects deep values and wisdom."

Now with clients across 14 countries at Mitha Aahara, Sreemathy with her team, which has grown over the past 5 years since its inception, has observed a universaltruth:

People always return to the food of their childhood-the meals that feel like home.

In her clinical practice, she designs personalized plans based on regional diets. "I must know whether it's a rasam, a kattu, or a tomato soup -each has emotional value, " she explains. She honours regional cuisines, avoids imposing Western diets, respects individual food preferences, and celebrates the natural balance of traditional Indian meals-while thoughtfully adapting them to the pace and convenience of modern life.

Her approach is firmly grounded in science, including the understanding that the gut micro biome is the seat of both health and disease-a truth long acknowledged in Indian wisdom and reflected in the teachings of the *Charaka Samhita*, which emphasises that all disease and healing begin in the gut. This reinforces how deeply traditional dietary patterns are connected to gut health and overall well-being.

Kitchen: The Heart of the Home

She believes that the kitchen has long been the heart of every home, where love and healing are passed down in the form of recipes and traditions.

"When a child falls sick, the first thing a mother or grandmother does is head to the kitchen not the medicine cabinet, " she says. "That's our instinct to heal with food."

She believes the crux of these lies in the age old traditions passed down by dadis and nanis to the generations. These hold timeless wisdom for health.

Key Diet Principles shared by Sreemathy

1. "The Indian micro biome project clearly shows that Indians naturally have a strong gut."
   She explained that our traditional diets made with fermented foods, lentils, millets and home cooked meals build a resilient gut ecosystem.

2. "We must eat more home cooked balanced meals, especially the food we grew up with."
   She emphasised that Indian bodies thrive on familiarity like dal and rice, sabzi, curd, millets, regional vegetables and culturally rooted meals.
3. "If you want to enjoy a sweet during a festival you should have it without guilt in moderation and then return to your regular home cooked meals."
   Her message was simple. Celebrations are part of life and guilt harms metabolism more than the sweet.
4. "Your food should be simple predictable and comforting and not confusing."
   She explained that fad diets disturb the gut while routine and consistency strengthen digestion.
5. "Our bodies are designed for cooked meals. Raw salads are not an Indian staple and do not suit everyone's gut."
   She suggested warm cooked and easy to digest food for daily eating.

Women of Today: The Balancing Act

"We are the bridge between two generations, " she says.

"We guide our children forward while holding our parents close." She calls today's generation the *sandwich generation*-carrying love in two directions.

"On one side are our children, growing up in a fast-paced, digital age. On the other are our parents, who come from a time when connection meant letters and face-to-face conversations."

"Even my parents managed this balance so gracefully, " she recalls. "But today, technology has become our ally. It's wonderful to see how it helps us stay close despite physical distances."

She believes caregiving is now shared, with men stepping into nurturing roles too, creating collaborative families rooted in support, values, and warmth.

Her own motherhood reflects this balance-taking 15 days off during her children's board exams, sitting outside the exam hall to reassure them, being present when it mattered most.

Key Advice to Women

1. "Do not feel guilty for taking a break because a pause in your life is not a failure."
2. "Prioritise your health with the same commitment you give to your family."
3. "Eat on time and nourish yourself because your body cannot pour from an empty cup."
4. "Respect your hormonal changes and adjust your lifestyle gently instead of forcing extreme diets."
5. "Create boundaries and protect your mental space since self care is strength and not selfishness."

If you want, I can also create a short box titled Her Advice to Every Woman for your chapter.

Entrepreneurship with a Purpose

In the next phase of her journey, she expanded Mitha Aahara into thoughtful products- moringa-infused ghee, moringa powders,

ABC juice mixes, and functional foods-each blending ancient wisdom with modern nutritional science.

Her goal remains simple:

Health should be doable, accessible, and rooted in familiar flavours.

A Journey Rooted in Care

Sreemathy's journey stands as a quiet but compelling reminder that real change begins at home, in the choices we make and the care we offer. **From her early years of service as a clinical dietitian to her purposeful leap into entrepreneurship with Mitha Aahara, she has carried one unwavering belief: good health should not be complicated.** Her work continues to touch lives through simple, truthful nutrition and the compassion behind it. In every consultation, every product and every message she shares, Sreemathy shows that nurturing others is not just her profession but her lifelong calling. She is truly a *Nurturer Draped in a Saree*.

CHAPTER 11

SOULFIRE DRAPED IN A SAREE: MINI GYAN GAUTAM, CORPORATE LAWYER

> *"The world expects out of a woman the power of ten hands and five brains all at once. But we always rise to the occasion because that is what gives us our purpose."*

Mini Gyan Gautam is a corporate lawyer by profession, but at heart she is someone whose instinct is to help. She believes that the true power of law lies not in authority but in service. **Over the past fifteen years, she has carved a distinct niche for herself in Intellectual Property and Entrepreneurial Law, fields in which her firm, Arthavat Law Offices, now specialises**. Before starting her own firm, she worked with the National Stock Exchange in Mumbai and later with L and T Financial Services, gaining invaluable experience across corporate and regulatory law.

Her excellence has been recognised widely. **She was named among India's Top 40 Lawyers under 40 by Business World** and **featured in iPleaders' list of the Top 100 Lawyers to Follow on LinkedIn.** She has also been invited by numerous colleges to mentor students and aspiring lawyers. Yet beyond every award, what defines Mini most deeply is her humanity. She often says that law must stand beside people, not above them. "Law gives me an edge. The ability to empower others, by helping them understand their rights. That's what truly matters to me, " she reflects with conviction.

The Girl Who Watched the World Carefully

Mini's journey began at La Martinière for Girls in Kolkata, where even as a science student her voice, presence, and articulation set her apart. **She thrived in debates and elocutions and often expressed herself through poetry.** Her English teacher, Mrs B Banerjee, recognised her gift early. "Mini you are gifted. You don't just speak well, you speak from the heart, " she would say.

Everything changed in Class Eleven when the horrific rape and murder of a minor by Dhananjoy Chatterjee shook her city. The case awakened something fierce in her, a desire to stand for what was right. The national debate felt personal and defining. The entire news headlines in print media and on news channels debating over capital punishment really influenced her decision to take up law.

Her father, an IAS officer, and mother shaped her emotional intelligence and moral grounding. They taught her that strength must always be paired with empathy. This became the philosophy she carries into her practice even today.

When Destiny Whispered

After deciding to pursue law, Mini appeared for multiple entrance exams including NLS Bangalore, NALSAR Hyderabad, NLIU Bhopal, Symbiosis Pune, and ILS Pune. Though selected by Symbiosis, **she chose ILS for its academic excellence. Destiny aligned itself quietly when her future husband also shifted to ILS the same year.**

Later she went on to pursue corporate law at King's College in London along with Anshuman, her then partner and now husband. At King's, she experienced true equality and integrity in the legal system. The exposure strengthened her belief that justice must be rooted in fairness. She often recalls how in London, women were treated as equals and the law respected integrity above all.

Law That Breathes Through Everyday Life

For Mini, law has always been about clarity and common sense. **"To me, law is not rocket science. It is logical, practical, and deeply human, "** she often says.

Her legal training empowered her far beyond the courtroom.

What she cherishes most is the ability to help - to simplify, to advise, and to empower. For Mini, being a lawyer is not just a profession but a way of giving back - using understanding and reason to bring a little more justice into everyday life. **From a very young age, she was aware of her rights and unafraid to assert them.** Though she practices corporate law today, she believes that everyone deserves access to basic legal guidance, something she readily offers whenever she can.

One incident stays with her even today. She once accompanied her nanny, who was being abused, to the police station to help her file a complaint. It reinforced her belief in the system. "I've never been afraid of the police. They are there to help, " she says.

That day she realised the law is not something to fear but a tool to protect.

Her knowledge became her quiet strength, helping her support neighbours, friends, and even strangers who needed guidance.

A Bond Rooted in Respect

Her relationship with her husband Anshuman Chanda, who is also a corporate lawyer, blossomed naturally from friendship into love during law school. Studying together for their master's degree gave them time to understand each other beyond academics. **Their bond is rooted in shared values, mutual respect, and a deep understanding of each other's profession**. When they returned to India, marriage felt like the most natural step.

Never Too Late to Rise

Mini firmly believes in reinventing oneself at any age. **"Even if you begin later in life, you can always learn, grow, and build something meaningful, "** she says with quiet conviction.

Her father in law started practicing law at fifty five, strengthening her faith in lifelong learning.

She knows of a lady who became a real estate agent in her 50s, by gaining knowledge about the field and starting her own practice.

She often wonders why more women cannot do the same. "It made me think. Why aren't more women doing the same?" she reflects.

The answer, she realised, lies in the lack of childcare support. **"In cities like Delhi, Mumbai, or Bangalore, there are good day cares. But in smaller towns it's a struggle, "** she explains.

Without support systems, women cannot return to full time work or further studies.

She from her own experience confirms that day cares need to be improved for more women to join work again.

A Life Built on Courage and Choice

For Mini, working independently was not rebellion but a deeply personal choice. Flexibility played a defining role in her journey as a mother and professional. "Flexibility helps you as a parent too, " she says simply.

When her daughter recently developed a bacterial infection and had to stay home for nearly a week, Mini managed both caregiving and work without stress. "If I had been in a full-time role, that would have been a major problem, " she admits.

But this time, she could balance everything. "It didn't make a difference to me. I could be there for her and still manage my work."

Her pregnancy too was challenging, requiring two months of bed rest, yet she navigated it with resilience.

When her daughter was born, Mini made a conscious decision.

"I didn't want my daughter to grow up thinking her father drives and her mother cooks. I wanted her to see that both can do both."

This became symbolic of the equality she wanted to model at home.

Mini balances motherhood and career with great confidence. **Her choices may appear small - learning to drive, trusting a day care, sharing caregiving duties - but each one chips away at deep-rooted stereotypes.** Through her actions, she is shaping a new definition of strength: one where equality begins at home.

Breaking Bias with Every Step

As Mini grew in her profession, she became increasingly aware of the gender imbalance that persists across industries. "On a larger scale, women are not invited or welcomed in most fields, " she observed with honesty.

This statement reflects her lived experience and the quiet barriers women face daily. She also spoke about how artificial intelligence mirrors societal prejudice.

"When AI is asked to search for a teacher's picture, it'll show a woman. And if you search for an engineer, it'll show a man, " she explains.

According to her, these patterns reveal what the world still unconsciously believes: that women belong in caregiving roles while men belong in technical or leadership roles.

Media reinforces this divide.

"There are so many advertisements that are so offensive. In a cooking advertisement they'll show the mother. And in an insurance advertisement they'll show the father, " she points out. These images quietly shape how society views gender and responsibility. Another bias she encounters is around maternity leave.

"If a woman takes maternity leave, companies feel they will have to pay without getting work. So they prefer not to hire women at all, " Mini says candidly.

She believes this is one of the reasons women are still not represented fairly.

"That's the reason why women are not being represented well enough in the corporate culture, " she concludes. Workplace safety is especially close to her heart. She is firm when she says, "As per law, every organisation is required to have a POSH committee. It's not optional." Yet she often hears people dismiss it with casual remarks like, "No complaint has come, so we don't have to do it."

These experiences strengthened her resolve to advocate for women with even more determination.

Carving Her Own Path

The decision to start a legal consultancy did not come suddenly. It grew steadily over years of experience across sectors. She gained knowledge, credibility, and confidence while working with major corporates. The birth of her law firm Arthavat brought her independence and flexibility in thought as well as time management. But the journey into independence was still daunting.

"It was always a question mark. When your parents are not from the legal field, how do you get clients? How do you generate revenue?" she says with a thoughtful smile.

Those questions felt heavy in the beginning.

She noticed that in many places, people approached lawyers only when a crisis occurred.

"**Many people think of going to a lawyer only when something goes wrong. They don't see legal compliance as part of building a responsible business**, " she explains. Her first step was founding her consultancy in Delhi. Later she moved to

Goa, where she found a healthier work life balance. One of the reasons she learned driving was safety during late work hours.

For her, safety and dignity were as important as professional growth. Slowly and steadily, she built her identity as a lawyer who cares, a lawyer who listens, and a lawyer who acts.

A Legacy Written in Kindness

Mini is not just a corporate lawyer. For her it is about leaving behind a legacy where she is remembered as someone who helped others- it's about people. She believes her sense of justice, and her desire to reach out to those in need all come from her father.

Her father, a bureaucrat, wasn't remembered for his title or authority, but for his goodness. **Among countless officers, people still talk about him - not because of what he achieved, but because of how he made them feel.** Every morning, he would call people who needed help be it friends, family, even strangers and ask, "How can I help you today?" It wasn't duty; it was who he was. His warmth, his kindness, and his readiness to serve left a lasting mark on Mini's heart.

She asserts she has inherited those qualities from him. In her own way, she tries to carry forward his legacy every day. Though she practices corporate law, her purpose goes far beyond boardrooms and contracts. She devotes her time to helping people who can't afford good legal aid -those who often fall through the cracks of the justice system.

This, she says, is the legacy she wants to leave behind, to be remembered not just as a successful lawyer, but as someone who stood by people when they needed help the most.

Mini has always advocated for equality. **She has been a person who has reached out to people emotionally even when they weren't close to her**. She is a dynamic lawyer; there are no two ways about that. But above it all she has a soul that stirs when someone is wronged-A heart that wants to use knowledge not just to build empires but to help people get justice. Mini is truly a *Soul Fire Draped in a Saree.*

CHAPTER 12

RESSURECTION DRAPED IN A SAREE: PRERNA KARIDHAL, ENTREPRENEUR

"Entrepreneurs have this thing within them, they are born with extreme optimism. It might not suit everyone but that is who I am."

In a world where women are so often taught to be "pretty" before "brave", Prerna Karidhal quietly defied that expectation. The words of the poet Katie Makkai-"You will never be merely pretty"- could well describe the spirit with which Prerna walked her own path. **Today she stands tall as the founder of QUREZ, a PETA certified, vegan and cruelty free skin care brand, that champions clean beauty and conscious living** – a brand that has won numerous accolades for its ethical innovation and honesty. For her transformative work and her unwavering commitment to purposeful entrepreneurship, **she was honored with the Rex Karamveer Chakra Award**. Her story, however, didn't begin in the world of serums and sunscreens, but amidst machines, steel and ambitions as tough as iron.

Discovering her Grit

A mechanical engineer from the prestigious Indira Gandhi Institute of Technology (IGIT) (2012), Delhi, Prerna was never the one to blend in the background. In college she was elected the Vice President of SAE IGIT, where she led her team, in designing a breakthrough model of a light weight formula car, for which they were **felicitated by the then Chief Minister of Delhi- a moment that revealed her passion for creating something**.

Even before she had a degree in hand she began her entrepreneurial conquest with BagYourBook, a student venture that made educational books accessible and affordable, making her first tryst with innovation.

Learning the System

Initially she treaded the conventional path as she began her professional career with Hindustan Unilever. **She worked in the Supply Chain Department. Here she learned about organization structure**. She was a woman in a male dominated company but she stood her ground. She showed that she had the rigor to handle operations and creativity to bring fresh ideas to the table; rare blend of balanced nuances.

A New Beginning and a Quiet Love Story

But the hum of machines soon gave way to the pulse of ideas. She moved into the startup arena with CarDekho and Jabong, spaces that offered her what she valued the most-creative freedom. In both these companies she grew as a person and as an entrepreneur. This was also the period when her long friendship turned into a lifelong bond. Prerna had known her husband Sanjay since their college days, where he had been her steady confidante, someone who understood her dreams without judgment**. Over the years, through career shifts and life's turns, their companionship only deepened.** When she was working at CarDekho, they finally decided to tie the knot, not out of haste but out of years of trust and shared purpose.

The Night that changed her Life

In the year following her beautiful wedding, while travelling with her mother in law and husband to take care of a personal tragedy, **during the late hours at night, their car met with an accident.** Life flashed in front of her eyes, as she lay there in a pool of blood with her husband and mother in law in dire conditions.

"You are strong, gather yourself up"

She told herself.

The gruesome reality of the world was right in her face as people stole from them instead of helping. She somehow got hold of her phone and called her parents as well as the hospital nearest to their highway spot. **They were saved, as she believed, by a**

Divine Power. A power that held her through the recuperation that followed this tragic incident.

Rising from Within

In her time away from her work life, at home with her husband and family members, **Prerna began a retrospection of her journey**; the past grit, the diligence and the path ahead. The near death experience made her realize how unexpected life could be. She wanted to do so much that could have ended in that one night. So on one of those days when self-motivation was all she had she made the decision that changed the course of her life.

"**Life is too short and uncertain to leave any of your dreams unfulfilled. We must at least give it a try**." She says with a determined smile,

Being a quiet rebellion against the shallow definitions of beauty, her time in solitude ignited something profound within her. **What had started as personal blog born out of introspection and empathy slowly evolved into a vision.** The vision was to create nontoxic, environment friendly products that were honest and pure.

Qurez emerged, much like her, like phoenix rising from the ashes.

Battles beyond Ideas

Starting something of her own had never frightened Prerna- she had conviction and an idea that mattered. But as she would soon learn, having an idea and getting it funded were two very different battles. **The boardrooms and investor calls were rarely neutral spaces.** Time and again, she noticed a subtle, persistent disparity- investors seemed more confident betting on men than on women. Questions arose about her "long term plans" often carried unspoken undertones: *What if she gets married? What if she becomes a mother? Is she serious about her brand?*

For women, society still viewed milestones like marriage and motherhood as interruptions, not evolutions of ambition. Yet Prerna stood her ground. She refused to apologize for her dreams. What she lacked initially from institutional backing, she made up for in unyielding support from her immediate family.

Faith, Family and the First Big Order

One memory from those early days remains etched in her heart. **It was a rainy night in Delhi, and she was busy packing one of Qurez's very first bulk orders.** The brand was still in its infancy- there was no office, no formal set up, just boxes, labels and BELIEF. As the clock struck mid night, she realized she couldn't possibly deliver this with a handful of staff members. **To her surprise, her husband and mother in law rose to the occasion- from taping boxes, loading cartons and finally driving through the rain to the Amazon facility.** That night they returned home triumphant. "We sat for dinner at 2 in the morning." For Prerna it wasn't the size of the order that mattered- it was the warmth of that moment. It was proof that her dreams were not hers alone; they became her families shared faith.

A Mother's Promise to Protect

In the year 2021 when Prerna first became pregnant, her gynecologist gave her a surprising instruction; **"Please avoid sunscreen during pregnancy."** It seemed counterintuitive- why would something meant to protect the skin be forbidden in the most crucial days of a woman's life? But that question planted a seed of curiosity in her.As she moved through her pregnancy, and later into production of skincare and serums, Prerna began digging deeper, what she found shocked her. A large number of creams and sunscreens on the market contained UV filters, parabens, phenols and other chemical compounds many of which had not been studied adequately for safety in pregnancy and infants.

More alarmingly, she came across studies highlighting the environmental damage of some of these chemicals. **These were harmful to the coral reefs and marine organisms according to what she had researched.** The idea that sunscreen applied by someone could wash of entire ranges of coral reefs struck her as tragic and intolerable. (Reports in National Park Service website article dated August 11, 2022.)

Fueled by this revelation, Prerna redirected all her focus towards creating a truly nontoxic and **environmental friendly Sunscreen, safe for mothers and infants.** She set out to formulate a mineral-based, reef friendly sunscreen- one free of chemical UV filters and endocrine disruptors, one using zinc oxide or titanium dioxide (in safe forms), and one built from ingredients that wouldn't disrupt fragile bodies or fragile ecosystems.

In that moment, when her own pregnancy revealed the gap between what the market offered and what was safe, Prerna's mission crystalized; to fill it with a sunscreen that would protect without poisoning. Her brand Qurez would not only stand for beautiful skin – but for responsible, conscientious beauty that honors both human life and the planet we live on.

Home Is where the Heart Is

Today, Prerna Karidhal stands at the helm of Qurez- not just as its founder, but as its beating heart. She runs her brand with quiet determination, balancing board meetings with bed time stories, product launches with school lunches. As a devoted mother, she built an office space just a few steps away from her home- a symbol of how she has merged two worlds that society often tells women to keep apart.

Mother in Laws Faith

Yet, what truly anchors her journey is the bond she shares with her mother in law. **Prerna trusts her not only with her child but with her deepest dreams. Her mother in law had once cradled Qurez with faith and warmth** when it was fragile. Now she does the same with her grandchild. With support and relentless spirit, Prerna continues to expand Qurez- adding new nontoxic and environmental friendly products to its line. To her this is just the beginning of a long standing mission. The mission is not just to sell beauty products but to change certain beauty norms and redefine them.

Womanhood is Challenging and Rewarding

"Often woman have to balance both career and homes; it is difficult to manage without a good support system, " she says, pondering over the work life balance issues woman face these days. "**But if you ambitions are clear and you plan ahead of time, everything is possible**, " she says with a determined glint in her eyes. "And the rest of it, all I can say is that, take it as it comes." Her smile is that of a confident woman ready to conquer the world ethically and sustainably.

To the new age woman who want to be entrepreneurs she says, "Be compassionate along with being ambitious. **The true meaning of life is to do whatever you want to with full honesty and dedication, whether it is looking after your family, raising your children or having a career."** She would have never really found her true calling if not for that one gruesome incident she believes. According to her it was by the will of a higher being that she could live to build her life again. Hence, she requests humbly to everyone to fulfill their dreams even as they tread through mundane everyday lives.

Her story reminds us that incidents meant to break us can, in truth, remake us. Sometimes the most profound creations rise from the quietest struggles. A woman who build not only a brand but reasserted the fact that beauty can coexist with conscience. She resurrected herself, leading her to the glory that she deserves. She is truly resurrection, *Resurrection Draped in a Saree.*

CHAPTER 13

CONCLUSION: THE QUIET POWER OF WOMEN

When I began this book, I believed I was simply gathering stories. But as I walked alongside each woman, I realised they were not just sharing their journeys with me. They were shaping mine. Their experiences, their truths, their courage, all became gentle lessons resting in my heart.

These women, so unique in their paths yet united by a quiet inner fire, taught me that real strength is often silent. It rises softly, choosing purpose even in pain, and it carries love even when the world feels heavy. True courage is waking up one more day with hope.

While writing, I went through my own waves of emotion. There were days when I felt stretched thin between work, writing, children, and caring for my husband and other family members. I often sat at my desk late at night, exhausted, wondering how much more I could hold. In those moments I think to myself, this is exactly why I need to write this book even more. Women everywhere carry so much on their shoulders. I wanted this book to be a reminder that they are not alone.

There were moments when someone said that books like this already exist. Their words stung more than I expected. They did not understand that I was not writing to compete or to impress anyone. I was writing for the women who had lost hope. I was writing for the ones who need a voice whispering to them that strength still lives within them. In moments of doubt, I reminded myself whyi began to reach out, to encourage, to heal. Even if one woman feels seen because of this book, it is worth it.

At times, the emotions became overwhelming. I cried between paragraphs, sometimes from empathy, sometimes from exhaustion, sometimes because their stories mirrored the unspoken parts of my own. But maybe that is why this book feels alive. It was written with a heart that was overflowing. Some chapters broke me. Some healed me. And some held me like a quiet prayer.

As I continued writing, something almost sacred began to unfold. People appeared at just the right time. Conversations opened effortlessly. Words arrived when I thought I had none left. It felt like a gentle divine guidance holding me. As if the universe wanted these stories to be told. I often felt the planets silently aligning, pushing me forward with a kind of grace I cannot fully explain.

And somewhere in the middle of these pages, something new awakened in me.It is a mix of a spark, a vision, the beginning of another journey. It whispered of a book that would honour the nine roops of Goddess Durga through real women who help each other rise. That is how The Durga Chronicles was born in my heart-A continuation of this path, another offering of sisterhood and strength.

What touched me the most was the humanity of every woman in this book. Despite their achievements, their brilliance, their challenges, they remained warm, grounded, kind, and so deeply approachable. They shared their time freely. They spoke with honesty. They trusted me. They stood by me in the same quiet way women have always stood beside one another.

This is the greatest truth they taught me.

When women stand together, the world does not simply move forward. It transforms.

It grows softer. It becomes braver. It becomes a kinder place to belong.

This book began with a simple click when I did a three day class on "How to be an Author" from Inspiring Jatin. It was during the sessions that I realised that time bound work always gets done. If I would have procrastinated too much I would have never achieved this. I believe these stories chose me. And through them, I discovered parts of myself I had forgotten.

As I close this chapter, I carry with me a gratitude that rests quietly in my heart, for the trust these women placed in me, for the universe that aligned my steps, and for the unseen grace that held my hand through each page.

May their stories stay with you.

May they remind you of your own quiet power.

May they give you hope on the days you feel tired or unseen.

And may they prepare you for the stories waiting in The Durga Chronicles, where the spirit of sisterhood continues to shine.

This is not an ending. This is the beginning of many more stories that are waiting to be told.

ACKNOWLEDGEMENTS

My deepest gratitude goes to each extraordinary woman whose strength fills these pages. Thank you for trusting me with your journeys and for letting me step into the most intimate corners of your lives.

Paramjeet Choudhary, thank you for showing me how quiet dignity can hold enormous courage and how a mother's heart can rebuild entire worlds.

Mrs Sarkar, your grace, resilience and calm wisdom reminded me that leadership is not loud, it is steady and compassionate.

Dr Aruna Tantia, your dedication to healing and your ability to blend science with sensitivity taught me what true service looks like.

Anamika Ghose, your warmth, creativity and strength in the face of personal challenges showed me how beautifully a woman can rise again.

Dr Kaberi Kar Gupta, your clarity of purpose and your commitment to every cause you believe in inspired me throughout this journey.

Mini Gautam, your honesty, humour and raw vulnerability made me understand how powerful it is when a woman owns her story.

Rekha Sharma, your perseverance and the quiet power with which you navigated every obstacle left a lasting impression on me.

Manjari Sahai, thank you for showing me what elegance in resilience looks like and how strength can coexist with deep sensitivity.

Sreemathy Venkatraman, your passion for wellbeing and your determination to serve others through your knowledge truly moved me.

Prerna Karidhal, your brilliance, humility and fearless pursuit of dreams reminded me that the sky is never the limit for a determined woman.

I am deeply thankful to my professors and teachers who shaped my thinking and nurtured the values that guide my writing. To my students, who inspire me with their questions, their energy and their unfiltered belief in possibilities, thank you for keeping my spirit young.

To my seniors, your wisdom and encouragement often came to me at the exact moment I needed them. I am grateful for your steady presence. To my family, thank you for standing by me with love, patience and understanding as I balanced life, work and the emotional weight of writing these stories. Your faith in me kept me anchored.

To my friends who introduced me to these remarkable women and helped me build the bridges that made this book possible, thank you for believing in the power of these stories and for believing in me.

This book is a tapestry woven with support, kindness and the shared strength of every person mentioned here. I am deeply grateful to each one of you.

BIBLIOGRAPHY

The primary source of these journeys has been my interviews with these outstanding ladies, with their consent. But for the purpose of understanding their work better and describing them more efficiently these are the sources I have used. This is a non-exhaustive list but I have tried to mention all the sources clearly. If I have missed a source it is purely unintentional.

Chapter 3: Olympian Paramjeet Kaur

External Sources (With Links):

Asian Athletics Championships – Official Results Archive

https://www.worldathletics.org/competitions/asian-athletics-championships

(2000 Jakarta results referenced across athletics databases)

South Asian Games – Athletics Results & Records

https://www.sportsauthorityofindia.nic.in/sai/sag

(General athletics medal listings and athlete participation records)

Sydney Olympics 2000 – Official Relay Results (Women's 4×400m)

https://olympics.com/en/olympic-games/sydney-2000/results/athletics

(Includes team timings and national records)Athletics Federation of India – Athlete Performance Records & National Records

https://indianathletics.in/

Maharana Pratap Award – Rajasthan Government Sports Honours
https://sports.rajasthan.gov.in/
(Awardees listed under "Sports Awards" sections)
Aravali Award & Nahar Sanman Puruskar – Rajasthan State Award Information
https://www.rajasthan.gov.in/
(General state award listings; recipients vary by year)
Historical National Record (Women's 4×400m Relay) – PT Usha Era Statistics
https://www.worldathletics.org/records/
(Records comparison for India's relay teams)
Singapore Open Track and Field Championships – International Meet Archives
https://www.singaporeathletics.org.sg/
(Hosts archives and championship records for past events)
Media Coverage of Paramjeet Kaur's Olympic Participation and IRS Career Transition
https://www.thehindu.com/
https://timesofindia.indiatimes.com/
(Coverage of athletes entering civil services)

Chapter 4: Educationist Rupkatha Sarkar

External Sources (With Links):
La Martiniere for Girls, Kolkata – Official Website
https://www.lamartinieregirlskolkata.in/
Mother Teresa International Award for Education – Recipient Mentions & Coverage
https://www.motherteresaawards.org/

(General award listing; individual awardee pages vary by year)
IIHM Beacon of Excellence Award 2025 – Press Release & Coverage
https://www.iihm.ac.in/
(Award announcements appear under "News/Events" sections)
Presidency College (Now Presidency University), Kolkata – Official Website
https://presiuniv.ac.in/
St. Xavier's College, Kolkata – B.Ed Department Information
https://www.sxccal.edu/
St. Thomas' Girls School, Kolkata – School Overview
https://stthomasgirlsschool.com/
General media coverage on Mrs. Rupkatha Sarkar's role as Lady Principal, La Martiniere for Girls
https://www.telegraphindia.com/
(Contains multiple articles on her work and school leadership)
Articles on teaching excellence, pedagogy and education leadership in India
https://www.educationworld.in/
(Features on Indian educators including school principals)

Chapter 5: Dr. Aruna Tantia (ILS Hospitals)

External Sources (With Links):
ILS Hospitals – Official Website
https://www.ilshospitals.com/
(Institution founded under the leadership of Dr. Om Tantia and supported by Dr. Aruna Tantia)
ILS Hospitals – About Us (Institution History & Founders)
https://www.ilshospitals.com/about-us/

RNT Medical College, Udaipur – Official Information
https://education.rajasthan.gov.in/content/raj/education/rntmc–udaipur/en/home.html

Mata Gujri Memorial Medical College – Official Website
https://mgmmc.in/
(Institution where Dr. Aruna completed MS in Obstetrics & Gynecology)

Northwick Park Hospital (London North West University Healthcare NHS Trust)
https://www.lnwh.nhs.uk/northwick-park-hospital
(Where Dr. Aruna pursued her laparoscopy fellowship)

Anandlok Hospital, Kolkata – Hospital Information
https://www.anandlokhospital.com/

Mahavir Seva Sadan – Prosthetics and Philanthropy Organisation
https://www.mahavirsevasadan.com/

Rotary International – Community Service & Health Initiatives
https://www.rotary.org/

Women's Health & Laparoscopic Surgery (Contextual Reference for Technological Adoption in India)
https://www.fogsi.org/
(Federation of Obstetric and Gynaecological Societies of India)

Matri Raksha Project – Women's Menstrual Health Initiative (Referenced in public coverage of Kolkata health initiatives)
(Appears in multiple NGO and local coverage portals; official dedicated site not available)

Chapter 6: Dr. Kaberi Kar Gupta

External Sources (With Links):

Urban Slender Loris Project – Official Information / Conservation Details

https://www.lorisconservation.org/

(Contains references to global slender loris conservation including India's first long-term studies)

Paul Shin Award – Unsung Heroes of Science Education & Communication (2019)

https://www.nats.org/

(Award information referenced across science education organisations)

Wildlife Institute of India – Official Website

https://wii.gov.in/

(Institution where Dr. Kaberi completed her M.Sc and early research)

Kalakkad–Mundanthurai Tiger Reserve – Official Information

https://www.forests.tn.gov.in/pages/view/kalakkad-mundanthurai

(Primary site of her pioneering Slender Loris field research)

Research on Slender Loris Behaviour & Ecology – Academic References

https://scholar.google.com/

(Multiple academic papers authored/co-authored by Dr. Kaberi Kar Gupta)

North Carolina Museum of Natural Sciences – Research Associate Profile

https://naturalsciences.org/

(Institution Dr. Kaberi is affiliated with in the U.S.)

Biodiversity & Conservation Research (U.S. Academic Portals featuring her work)
https://researchgate.net/
(Youth mentoring, research collaborations and ecological studies)
General references on wildlife crime and turtle trade in India
https://wccb.gov.in/(Wildlife Crime Control Bureau – information related to illegal turtle trade networks)
Arunachal Pradesh – Bird & Wildlife Research (Background to her early work)
https://forest.arunachal.gov.in/

Chapter 7: Rekha Sharma

External Sources (With Links):
CCI Logistics Ltd. – Official Website (CSR Division & East Zone Initiatives)
https://www.cci-logistics.com/
CCI Logistics CSR Programs – Public Coverage & Press Releases
https://www.adgully.com/
(Features news on corporate CSR activities across India)
News Coverage of Transgender Community Events in Kolkata
https://www.telegraphindia.com/
(Reports on inclusivity initiatives and annual pre-Durga Puja homage events)
Coverage of Transgender Rights & Inclusion in India (General Context)
https://timesofindia.indiatimes.com/
(Articles on transgender community welfare and CSR participation)

Nari Sashaktikaran Sangrah – Women Empowerment & Social Work
(NGO is referenced widely in local coverage; no official website exists yet)
https://www.aninews.in/
(Used for tracking NGO-driven social programs and humanitarian outreach)
CSR India / National CSR Network – Documentation on Corporate Social Responsibility in India
https://www.csr.gov.in/
(Government portal listing corporate CSR activities and guidelines)
Social Welfare & Inclusion Reports (Government of West Bengal)
https://wb.gov.in/
(Reference for state-level social support and inclusion frameworks)
Media Coverage of Inclusivity Movements in East India
https://www.ndtv.com/
https://www.hindustantimes.com/
Gender & Human Rights Resources – Transgender Welfare Policies in India
https://ncw.nic.in/
https://transgender.dosje.gov.in/
(Government-run portals documenting transgender rights and support schemes)

Chapter 8: Anamika Ghose

External Sources (With Links):
The British School, New Delhi – Official Website
https://www.british-school.org/

Pathways World School, Aravali – Official Website
https://www.pathways.in/aravali
The Doon School, Dehradun – Official Website
https://www.doonschool.com/
St. Thomas' Day School, Kolkata – School Overview
https://stdayschool.org/
Loreto House School, Kolkata – Official Website
https://loretohousekolkata.com/
Pratt Memorial School – Official Information
https://prattmemorialschool.com/
Fergusson College (Now FC College, Pune) – Official Website
https://www.fergusson.edu/
Calcutta University – Department of Psychology
https://www.caluniv.ac.in/academic/psychology/
Oral School for Deaf Children, Kolkata – Institution Information (Listed under special schools in West Bengal archives)
https://wbped.gov.in/special-schools/
Telegraph School Awards for Excellence – Official Coverage
https://www.telegraphindia.com/
(Covers the 2000 Telegraph Award received by Anamika)
Centre of Assessments for Excellence – Award Announcements
(Includes "Exemplary Educator During Unprecedented Times Award 2020")
http://www.coe-believe.org/
Dr. Radhakrishnan Award (Education Sector) – Public Listings & Coverage
https://www.educationworld.in/
Information on ADHD & Child Psychology (Professional Reference)

https://www.aafp.org/
(General child development and ADHD understanding)
IBDP / International Baccalaureate Curriculum
https://www.ibo.org/
(Framework referenced in her work supporting students with special needs)
General resources on Neurodiversity and child counselling
https://childmind.org/

Chapter 9: Manjari Sahai

External Sources (With Links):
Enhance Designers – Official Business Information & Portfolio
(Firm co-created by Manjari Sahai; online references available through design listings)
https://www.indiamart.com/enhance-designers/
Times Design Ikons East Awards – 2025 Winners & Coverage
https://timesofindia.indiatimes.com/
(Coverage of design awards and East India design recognitions)
Berger Paints India (formerly British Paints) – Color & Training Resources
https://www.bergerpaints.com/
Loyola School, Jamshedpur – Official Website
https://www.loyolaschooljamshedpur.in/
Hindustan Development Corporation – Historical Business Information
(General reference for Kolkata-based industrial families)
https://www.zaubacorp.com/
Tega Industries Ltd. – Corporate Website
https://www.tegaindustries.com/

(Her uncle's company where early design opportunities emerged)
Spencer's Retail (Historical Background & Corporate Ownership)
https://www.spencers.in/
Pan Asia Restaurants – Design & Hospitality Projects in India
(Reference to one of her notable design contributions)
https://www.zomato.com/kolkata/pan-asian-restaurant
(General listing, project references vary by city)
General Design & Architecture Information (India's Interior Design Community)
https://www.architecturaldigest.in/
Women in Interior Design – Professional Insights & Industry Trends
https://www.designersguild.co.in/8

Chapter 10: Sreemathy Venkatraman

External Sources (With Links):
Mitha Aahara – Official Website
https://mithaaahara.com/
Sreemathy Venkatraman – Official Instagram (Nutrition Content & Product Updates)
https://www.instagram.com/sreemathyvenkatraman/
Global Conference & Awards 2025 – Excellence & Leadership in Healthcare
(Coverage of "Most Iconic Women of the Year in Nutrition & Dietetics")
https://www.healthcareglobal.com/
Golden Aim Awards – Healthcare Excellence (Online Nutrition Consultant Category)
https://goldenaimawards.com/

Michael Donavan Award – Advocacy Leadership in Dysphagia (Clinical Resources)
(Award referenced in dysphagia advocacy programs)
https://www.nationalfoundationofswallowingdisorders.org/
Christian Medical College, Vellore – Official Information
https://www.cmch-vellore.edu/
Femina Magazine – Articles Featuring Sreemathy Venkatraman
https://www.femina.in/
Times of India – Health & Nutrition Coverage
https://timesofindia.indiatimes.com/
NDTV Food – Expert Nutrition Interviews & Health Features
https://www.ndtv.com/food
Master's Program in Diet & Health – General Academic Reference
https://www.nutritionalstudies.org/
General Sources on Dysphagia & Clinical Dietetics
https://www.eatright.org/
https://www.ncbi.nlm.nih.gov/
Indian Microbiome Project – Gut Health Research Reference
https://www.ncbi.nlm.nih.gov/pmc/articles/PMC5330699/

Chapter 11: Mini Gyan Gautam

External Sources (With Links):
Arthavat Law Offices – Official Website
https://arthavat.com/
Business World – Top 40 Under 40 Lawyers List
https://www.businessworld.in/
(Features the "India's Top 40 Lawyers Under 40" selection where Mini was recognised)
iPleaders – Top 100 Lawyers to Follow on LinkedIn

https://blog.ipleaders.in/

V. G. Patel Memorial Awards – Entrepreneurship Support & Recognition

https://www.ied.edu.in/

(Institute of Entrepreneurship Development)

La Martinière for Girls, Kolkata – Official School Website

https://www.lamartinieregirlskolkata.in/

ILS Law College, Pune – Official Website

https://ilslaw.edu/

Symbiosis Law School – Entrance & Academic Information

https://www.symlaw.ac.in/

NLS Bangalore (National Law School of India University)

https://www.nls.ac.in/

NALSAR University of Law, Hyderabad

https://www.nalsar.ac.in/

Kingston University, London – Corporate Law Program Information

https://www.kingston.ac.uk/

National Stock Exchange of India – Corporate Information

https://www.nseindia.com/

L&T Financial Services – Corporate Website

https://www.ltfs.com/

POSH (Prevention of Sexual Harassment) Act – Government Guidelines

https://wcd.nic.in/act/sexual-harassment-women-workplace

(Referenced in her statements on workplace safety requirements)

Indian Legal Resources on Corporate & Entrepreneurial Law

https://www.barandbench.com/

https://www.livelaw.in/

Gender Bias in AI & Media – Public Discussion Resources
https://www.unwomen.org/
https://www.weforum.org/

Chapter 12: Prerna Karidhal (Founder, Qurez)

External Sources (With Links):
Qurez – Official Website (Products, Mission & Clean Beauty Philosophy)
https://qurez.com/
Qurez – Official Instagram (Brand Updates & Ingredient Transparency)
https://www.instagram.com/qurezindia/
PETA India – Certified Vegan & Cruelty-Free Brands List
https://www.petaindia.com/living/beauty-products/
(Verification of Qurez as a cruelty-free brand)Rex Karamveer Chakra Awards – Global Fellowship & Award Information
https://www.icarmaasia.org/
(Platform listing Karamveer Chakra awardees and social impact contributors)
Indira Gandhi Institute of Technology (IGIT), Delhi – Mechanical Engineering Program
http://www.igit.ac.in/
SAE India – Collegiate Club Projects & Formula Car Initiatives
https://www.saeindia.org/
BagYourBook – Early Student Venture (Archived References)
https://www.startupstorymedia.com/
(Lists early-stage student entrepreneurship in India)
Hindustan Unilever Limited – Corporate Website
https://www.hul.co.in/

CarDekho – Corporate Website
https://www.cardekho.com/
Jabong (Archived Business Information)
https://yourstory.com/2016/09/jabong-abof-aditya-birla
(Since Jabong was acquired and later shut down; references remain in business archives)
National Park Service (USA) – Article on Sunscreen Chemicals Impacting Coral Reefs (Aug 11, 2022)
https://www.nps.gov/articles/000/sunscreen-damage-coral-reefs.htm
Scientific Resources on Mineral Sunscreens & UV Filters
https://www.ncbi.nlm.nih.gov/
https://www.ewg.org/skindeep/
Athlete / Consumer Safety References on Pregnancy-safe Skincare
https://www.acog.org/
(American College of Obstetricians and Gynecologists)
Environmental Impact of Chemical Sunscreens – Global Research Summary
https://www.globalchange.gov/
Women Entrepreneurship & Startup Ecosystem in India
https://www.inc42.com/ (General background on funding disparity and women-led startups)

Notes

Notes